Davenport's Indiana Wills And Estate Planning Legal Forms

DAVENPORT'S INDIANA WILLS AND ESTATE PLANNING LEGAL FORMS

written by attorneys
Alex Russell and Robert Maxwell

Published by Davenport Publishing

**BOOK AND FORMS FREE AT
WWW.DAVENPORTPUBLISHING.COM**

COPYRIGHT © 2023 -- ALEX RUSSELL

CREATIVE COMMONS LICENSE. This work is also licensed under a Creative Commons Attribution-NonCommercial-NoDerivatives 4.0 International License.

GOVERNMENT WORKS. No claim is made to copyright or ownership of government materials.

SOME STANDARD FORMS. No copyright or ownership is claimed of "standard" forms or leading forms for the state which are provided in this book, but fair use and privilege to use is claimed. Makers of such forms (often state agency or hospital) have agreed by word, action, inaction, and implication forms may be used and copied if no profit is sought and no substantial changes made. Such makers if not lawyer or law firm are barred from profit or advantage through practicing law by making forms then limiting use. Authors believe in a religious duty to help people and do charity.

PUBLICATION DATA

(informal, library may use different data)

Names: Russell, Alex, 1972- author ; Maxwell, Robert, 1960- author

Title: Davenport's Indiana Wills And Estate Planning Legal Forms

Other Titles: Davenport's Wills

Description: Davenport Publishing 2023

Suggested Identifiers: 9798374840476, LCCN 2021909030, 9798748423373

Subjects: LCSH: Wills--United States;
　　　　　　　　Wills--United States--Forms;
　　　　　　　　Estate Planning--United States;
　　　　　　　　Legal Forms

Classification:　　LFF KF755 .C55 2022 (or as library chooses)
　　　　　　　　DDC 346.73 Rus--dc23 (or as library chooses)

9 8 7 6 5 4 3 2 1 0 0 0 0 0 2 3

PERMISSION TO COPY AND USE BOOKS FOR FREE

To help people and groups publisher and authors of the book allow mostly free use by giving all a "Creative Commons Attribution-NonCommercial-NoDerivatives 4.0 International License". Basically as image below shows copying or use is OK if it still shows it's **by** the named authors, is **non-commercial** with no price charged, and has **no derivatives** which means no big changes. Most users face no limit on copying, using, holding in library to loan out, and giving out copies. Permission is given to change margins and formatting, do small changes, and cut any blank pages that may occur (but double-check page numbers and table of contents page numbers). Printing on only 1 side of paper pages may be best to not have complication of writing on back. Margins can be equal 0.76 inches, or for booklet 0.82 inch inside / 0.7 inch outside margins. Email questions to **davenportpress@gmail.com**.

(This work licensed under a Creative Commons Attribution-NonCommercial-NoDerivatives 4.0 International License.)

FOR FREE COPIES USE WWW.DAVENPORTPUBLISHING.COM OR BUY AT AMAZON.COM.

WARNING

THIS PUBLICATION IS NOT A SUBSTITUTE FOR LEGAL ADVICE. Publisher and authors say and warn this publication is not giving any legal, accounting, or other professional services or advice, which if wanted can be obtained by consulting in person an attorney or some other professional. **No attorney-client relationship or any relationship creating a duty or obligation is agreed to or created by the purchase or use of this publication or forms.**

CHAPTER	TABLE OF CONTENTS	PAGE NUMBER
1 - BOOK BASICS AND LIST OF FORMS		1
2 - TERMS, PROPERTY, AND HELPFUL INFORMATION FORM		4
3 - WILL BASICS		9
4 - WILL GIFTS INCLUDING RESIDUE		11
5 - DEBT, MARRIAGE, AND YOUNG CHILD ISSUES		15
6 - BASIC IDEAS ABOUT HEALTH CARE FORMS		18

AFTER DEATH FORMS

7 - FORM 1: WILL (STANDARD)		19
8 - FORM 2: WILL (GUARDIANS)		23
9 - FORM 3: SELF-PROVING CLAUSE		27
10 - FORM 4: TANGIBLE PERSONAL PROPERTY LIST		29

HEALTH CARE FORMS

11 - FORM 5: ADVANCE DIRECTIVE		31
12 - FORM 6: LIVING WILL DECLARATION		34
13 - FORM 7: DO NOT RESUSCITATE		36

GIVING POWER FORMS

14 - FORM 8: POWER OF ATTORNEY		41
15 - FORM 9: DELEGATION TO CONSENT TO HEALTH CARE OF MINOR CHILD		43
16 - FORM 10: FUNERAL PLANNING DECLARATION		45

APPENDIX: SAMPLE FILLED OUT FORMS		48

CHAPTER 1
BOOK BASICS AND LIST OF FORMS

ESTATE PLANNING CONTROLS THINGS IF LATER ABSENT, SICK, OR DEAD
From Davenport Publishing and written by attorneys this book covers "Estate Planning", about doing legal documents to later control health care, property, money, children, funeral, and more if absent, sick, or dead.

INDIANA LAW APPLIES TO PEOPLE LIVING HERE OR RETURNING
This book is for Indiana, and due to different laws an Estate Planning book and legal forms can't be used for a different state. Indiana law in this area applies if a person: a) <u>resides here</u> as their main home, or b) resided here and <u>left with firm plans to return</u> even if person rents a home elsewhere like some students, military, and workers. For health care forms people should <u>do forms to match state a health facility is in.</u>

BOOK IS SHORT, HAS FORMS TO QUICKLY SEE, AND USES EMPHASIS
This book by attorneys is <u>short so may read rough but lets person read in day the basics of the subject</u>. The book also has ready-to-use legal forms people can quickly see and use. For emphasis paragraph titles, <u>underlining</u>, and boxes are used. To save space some small words are skipped and end quotation marks put before punctuation. This book capitalizes some legal words like Will, Testator, and Agent but this is optional.

PEOPLE CAN IN FEW WAYS GET FORMS TO FILL OUT
To get forms to use people can 1) photocopy pages from book, 2) tear or cut out pages from book, or 3) at www.davenportpublishing.com get computer files to print (PDF is best option to avoid format changes). Usually legal forms use blank spaces to show where to add in words, like "I give _____ to _____". It is often fine to leave many blank spaces in forms unfilled, like people may skip using many Will gift spaces.

LEGAL SYSTEM IN ESTATE PLANNING ASKS WHAT DID PERSON WANT DONE
People have a legal right to control their health care, property, money, and family issues, and so judges, doctors, and others mostly just ask: **"Based on what a person wrote what did they likely want done?"** Neatness or nice wording is not needed. This book does explain what requirements documents do have.

FORMS ARE BINDING LEGAL DOCUMENTS AND DO SIMPLE THINGS WELL
Estate Planning research shows a shocking 60% of people die without doing anything, 19% use a lawyer, and 21% use legal forms. To help legal forms can be used more. Legal forms are good at most things involved and make binding legal documents judges, doctors, families, banks, and others must follow.

BOOK PROVIDES INDIANA "STANDARD FORM" OR SUITABLE FORM
Often an Indiana agency, hospital, or the legislature has made a form that most people in the state use and call the "standard form", and doctors, judges, and others may not like to follow a different form. To help this book <u>does</u> provide the standard state form in legal area if it exists, and in other areas authors provide a suitable form. A form put in law by state legislature to use if wanted is called a "statutory form".

BOOK COVERS LAW MOST PEOPLE WANT AND SOME STATE DIFFERENCES

This book covers what most people want to know. State laws are fairly similar in America and this book covers the most important American legal ideas. The book also covers major ways Indiana law is different. After reading this book some people may want to do their own research in the law.

THIS BOOK SHOULD SUIT PEOPLE WITHOUT STRANGE SITUATIONS OR WISHES

This book and its forms can't cover every issue that matters to everyone but it should suit people without strange situations or wishes about Estate Planning, which is probably most people and maybe over 80%. Strange situations or wishes that may need more research or a lawyer include: a) unusual wishes for gifts, b) wealth over $2 million, c) big medical concerns in family, d) property or money going to person with disability or "special needs", or e) wish to hide or move assets to quickly qualify for government programs. Many people re-do forms about each decade as their lives change.

ESTATE PLANNING OFTEN IS NOT VITAL

Despite what people may be told Estate Planning is usually not vital and worth much time or money. It usually does not: cut taxes unless person is a multi-millionaire, create new wealth, cut legal costs much, cut delay much, affect health care unless a person is suddenly incapacitated and rush decision needed, or affect children since tragedies are rare and if needed judges and families usually can act if needed. For young adults or parents the benefits of costly Estate Planning seem low since only about 9% of people die before 60, and only 0.2% of children under 19 had 2 parents die to probably ever need a Guardian. See Social Security Census Tables by Felicitie Bell; Life Factors & Mortality Study, Census Study 288.

INSURANCE MAY HELP MORE THAN COSTLY ESTATE PLANNING BY LAWYER

Instead of forms a lawyer can be paid to write complex Estate Planning documents but they can cost $1000s, take months, and make mistakes. In life people weigh costs and benefits and risks and often go with lower cost option. If people want to spend money in this area they can buy term life insurance of $100,000 via questionnaire but no exam ("simplified issue") for $50+a month or $400+ yearly from MetLife, State Farm, Haven, Ladder, SBLI, or AIG. Doing nothing and just saving money also can help family.

SOME LESS COMMON AND LESS USEFUL FORMS ARE NOT IN BOOK

This book skips less common or less useful documents.

A "Codicil" can modify a Will but most just re-do Will.

Some people do "Revocable Living Trust" so Trust entity with Trustee holds property or money, done mostly to after death avoid small delay, costs, and work (by "avoiding probate"). This is rarely done as it legally requires immediately moving items into a Trust with maybe years of hassle and costs, all for small later benefits for people who are probably happy to be getting things and don't mind minor work and delay.

"Childrens Trust" papers so a Trust upon a death then gets a minor child's money or property to manage until 18 is rare due to years of hassle and costs, and (as this book explains later) it rarely matters and most Wills already name Guardians and Custodian to help a child under 18.

Some people do a "Pet Trust" for money for pet, but it is easier to in a Will just give money along with pet.

Complex options may be suggested for estate tax reasons, but as this book explains few people owe this.

ESTATE PLANNING DOES SIMPLE THINGS IN 3 MAIN AREAS WITH 10 FORMS

Estate Planning seems complex but mostly is doing legal documents that mostly are in 3 areas: a) After Death, b) Health Care, and c) Giving Power. There are about 10 legal forms shown in this book. Most people do only 1 or 2 forms, like many people do 1 Will and 1 health care form, but some do more.

AFTER DEATH FORMS

Form 1. Will (Standard) – this Will lets a person control some things after their death like who gets their money and property, say who is Executor handling things, and letting some easier legal options be used later. **This Form 1 is the most used Will in the book and it suits most people.**

Form 2. Will (Guardians) – Will with parts added to name person as Guardian of Person to care for minor child under 18 if needed (like if no parent is available), and also name person as Guardian of the Estate to if needed manage money and property of a child and spend this on them till 18.

Form 3. Self-Proving Clause – done with Will to later help prove Will was properly signed.

Form 4. Tangible Personal Property List – lets person easily outside a Will write more gifts to occur after death of "tangible personal property" like cars, furniture, jewelry, tools, and clothes.

HEALTH CARE FORMS

Form 5. Advance Directive – lets person name Health Care Representative like family member or friend to control health care if person is later incapacitated and also write health care instructions (this form is often called a "Health Care Power Of Attorney"). **This Form 5 is often only health care form people use.**

Form 6. Living Will Declaration – does serious act of saying stop further health care if later doctors, think an incapacitated person's health is very bad and more care likely won't help.

Form 7. Do Not Resuscitate – does serious act of saying immediately from now on do not try C.P.R. to restart heart or breathing, and this short form that can be read fast is often used outside hospitals or similar (also provided in book is similar P.O.S.T. form covering more treatments than just C.P.R.).

GIVING POWER FORMS

Form 8. Power Of Attorney – lets power over money, property, and more be shared during life with trusted person named in form "Attorney-in-Fact" so they have legal power to help do things.

Form 9. Delegation To Consent To Health Care Of Minor Child – lets parent of child under 18 give power to someone over child's health care to make decisions if needed.

Form 10. Funeral Planning Declaration – lets instructions be given and if wanted a person named to control funeral and related issues (usually done if person doesn't want closest family for this like usual).

CHAPTER 2
TERMS, PROPERTY, AND HELPFUL INFORMATION FORM

THERE ARE BASIC TERMS AND IDEAS IN WILLS AND ESTATE PLANNING

Some legal terms and ideas are basic to Wills and Estate Planning.

■ "Estate Planning" is a person doing legal documents to control things if later absent, sick, or dead. After a form is signed a person is still free to sell or transfer property, instruct doctors, or change forms. The phrase "person doing a legal document" and "doing a form" means form is for and affects that person.

■ A person who died is called "decedent" or "deceased". Those getting Will gifts are often called "recipient", "beneficiary", or "heir" if related (they "inherit"). "Survive" or "surviving" is to be alive after the person named.

■ A "Will" or "will" (this book uses upper case "W") is a legal document done to control issues after death. The phrase "Last Will And Testament" is used since a "Testament" long ago was a small document done along with a Will to do some things. If no Will is done it is called being "intestate".

■ A person named to do things after someone's death is called by most people and this book "Executor", but in official papers and Wills the term "Personal Representative" is officially now used in Indiana.

■ A person doing a Will is called "Testator" or "Will maker". Long ago a woman Testator was called a "Testatrix" and woman Executor an "Executrix".

■ "Probate" is a legal process to do things after death like transfer property, authorize a Guardian, and handle creditors. Due to nice changes in law probate is now often "informal", faster, and less expensive.

■ "Property" is either: 1) "real property" which is land and buildings ("real estate"), 2) "personal property" which is things not real property, like cash, accounts, stocks, investments, tools, clothes, cars, jewelry, art, or 3) "fixtures" which are things tied to real property (like fences, posts, lighting, and wired-in appliances).

■ Forms to control things about health care are often called "Health Care Directives", but names vary.

■ Forms giving power are often named "Power of Attorney" forms, where a person called the "Principal" gives power to someone called the "Attorney-in-Fact" or "Agent".

■ State law is the Indiana Code and reference to a law can look like "Ind. Code 29-1-2-6" or "IC 29-1-2-6" to show the Title, Article, Chapter, and finally statute or section at issue (often the "§" symbol is used for statute or section). A legal form put in law for people to use if wanted is a "statutory form". Estate Planning mostly involves a local Circuit Court, and mostly involves Title 29 of state law which is called the "Probate Code".

LEGAL DOCUMENTS MAY NEED TO BE "WITNESSED" OR "NOTARIZED"

Legal documents to be valid may need to be "witnessed", which is someone watching person doing form sign it and then usually witness signs. Documents may need to be "notarized", which is person who is a "notary" (also called "notary public") see signing and use ink stamp on page and put their notary signature. This book explains for each form if witnesses or a notary is needed, and says who can be a witness. Notaries are found at some banks, brokers, insurance agents, courts, and government offices but they might be busy, decline to help, or they might only help existing customers. Notaries can be found in the phonebook.

ANYONE CAN FILL IN MOST OF FORM AND LATER TRY TO KEEP ORIGINAL

When filling out a form except for signature other parts can be filled in by person not doing document, maybe because of good handwriting or typing. After signing a form usually a person tries to keep the original and only hand out copies, though situations vary. Some people do "multiple originals" by having everyone sign identical documents to have many pages with real ink signatures, but this is rare and can be confusing.

"ESTATE" MEANS PROPERTY OF DECEDENT OR ENTITY HOLDING THINGS

The "Estate" or "probate estate" is all property and money of a person that on death did not somehow automatically transfer to other owners. "Estate" is also the word for the temporary entity run by Executor to do things after a death (sort of like a small corporation). A dead person's money and accounts might be renamed or moved to a bank account under an Estate name, like "Estate of John Eric Smith".

PROBABLY DO NEW FORMS IF DIVORCE, MARRY, HAVE CHILD, OR MOVE

Divorcing, marrying, having a new child, or moving to a new state can have big legal effects. If any of these events occur it is recommended people re-do a new Will and other Estate Planning papers soon. To help <u>most states say Will from another state is still valid</u>. Divorce does cancel Will gifts to an ex-spouse.

"INTESTATE" LAW SAYS WHERE THINGS GO AT DEATH IF THERE IS NO WILL

State "intestate law" says where property and money goes if no valid Will was done before person died (except for certain rights of spouses, family, and creditors). Intestacy laws often say half and sometimes all goes to any surviving spouse (if any), then half or any remainder goes to decedent's children natural or adopted (or if dead their child gets that share), then next closest family, and then the state. <u>Many people are happy with intestate law and intentionally die with no Will</u>, but many people do a Will to say who gets what.

PERSON CAN ONLY GIFT IN WILL WHAT THEY OWN AT DEATH

A person can only gift by Will things they own at death so people should research what they own.

Basically by law a person usually owns all they earn as wages and salary, owns their share of income and profit tied to property they own, and owns or partly owns any things their money buys or improves. But married people in Community Property law states might face different rules.

For property with "title" documents (real estate or vehicles) or where there is a "listed owner" (like accounts) the named persons are usually the legal owners unless evidence shows special circumstances.

Note, a person during life can sell property, make gifts, or transfer things even if items are named in a Will, so people should consider if they already sold or gave away property they also name in a Will gift.

THINGS OWNED IN SPECIAL WAYS MAY LIMIT WILL GIFTING

A person should consider if they own real estate or other property in special ways which may limit gifting by Will. Laws vary but some special joint ways are:

a) "joint tenant with right of survivorship" or similar so then property transfers automatically to the other named owners regardless of a Will, which in some states is often how a family house is held,

b) a "life estate" where papers say if life of someone ends the other people in papers get item, and

c) "Trust property" if paperwork made a Trust entity and property was actually transferred into it, so then the Trust papers control where things put in the Trust go on someone's death.

But normal joint property for the part owned <u>can</u> be gifted by Will, like "I give the half of Boat that I own with Aunt Jo to Ed Fox". Joint ownership can occur if people do joint papers, agree to own jointly, buy with joint funds, a gift is to multiple persons, or if married and in a Community Law state money or property is gained.

WARNING: "NON-PROBATE PROPERTY" TRANSFERS IGNORE ANY WILL

Money or property that for some reason automatically transfers on death to other owners is called "non-probate property", and such things quickly transfer as arranged even if a Will names the same items. Examples of non-probate property are: a) a "designated beneficiary" form done earlier names person to get account or investment, b) transfer-on-death account, and c) real estate like a house held by 2 people as "joint tenants with survivorship" or similar ways so survivor gets things. Property and money in a Trust also ignores a Will and transfers as trust papers say. Insurance with a beneficiary usually ignores a Will. Trying to do non-probate transfers for all things is called "avoiding probate", but it is rarely tried as it may make living and paperwork a hassle for years, benefits are small, and often a thing is missed anyway. <u>When doing a Will a person should consider non-probate transfers that will occur automatically on death and consider what property and money will be left to transfer by Will.</u>

USUALLY NO FEDERAL, INDIANA, OR OTHER TAX IS OWED AT A DEATH

Usually no tax is owed as a result of a death, including no estate, inheritance, death, or similar taxes. This is because the "Federal Estate And Gift Tax" only starts when a tax credit is used up that covers <u>$12.92 million per person in 2023</u> (with yearly rises for inflation). Also since 2013 Indiana law changes there are no Indiana estate or inheritance taxes that may be owed due to a death. Some states have inheritance taxes on things leaving their state but often they only start taxing at values over $3,000,000. <u>Usually only multi-millionaires in Indiana need to worry about additional taxes at death.</u>

SOME PEOPLE DO "HELPFUL INFORMATION" FORM

It is <u>not a real legal form that legally does anything but a person can do a "Helpful Information" form</u> so family or friends after person's death have more information about property, money, debts, and other things. Neatness is not needed and often person does it quickly, writes in more over time, and prints and attaches pages with info. The form is often kept with a Will and at death goes to Executor or family. <u>See next pages.</u>

ESTATE PLANNING HELPFUL INFORMATION

Give information to help family, friends, and Executor after your death. If needed attach more forms or blank pages.

1. Personal Information (Name, Birthdate, Social Security #, special family details, other):

2. Real estate, vehicles, and other tangible property of high value (especially if people may not find them):

3. Non-tangible assets like stocks, accounts, investments, loans owed you, and businesses of high value:

4. Possible income or insurance of high value like pensions, retirement, disability, insurance, or contracts:

5. Debts owed by you like credit card, loan, student loan, mortgage, vehicle loan, and accounts payable:

6. Names and contact information of professionals used (attorneys, accountants, brokers, doctors, others):

7. Computer passwords and helpful files, document places, and safes or safe-deposit boxes codes/keys:

8. Other helpful things, wishes for funeral, special requests, and any last messages to family and friends:

CHAPTER 3
WILL BASICS

WILL LETS "TESTATOR" CONTROL THINGS AFTER DEATH
A Will is a legal document done by a person who is called "Testator" or "Will Maker" to control some things after their death. Testator <u>when signing</u> must be at least 18, of sound mind (rational with sufficient memory), and not be under duress (unfair pressure or threat), and rarely can a person not do a Will.

SIGN WILL IN FRONT OF 2 WITNESSES WHO THEN SIGN

WILL TO BE VALID MUST BE WRITTEN AND SIGNED WITH 2 WITNESSES
To be a valid Will in Indiana it must show it is meant as a Will, be written, and be signed in front of 2 witnesses who sign too. A Will must be written on paper in some way. A "Video Will", "Audio Will", or online or computer Will is powerless. Verbal promises about things after death are mostly invalid if not in a Will. Some states but <u>not</u> Indiana let 2 witnesses be skipped if Will is all handwritten, called a "holographic" Will.

WITNESS MUST BE AT LEAST 18 AND USUALLY NOT NAMED IN WILL
<u>The 2 witnesses to Will signing can be anyone at least age 18 even a non-resident</u> but it is preferable they not be too old or living too far away. If a person is getting a Will gift <u>they can be a witness</u> but the gifts are void and canceled except close family can get up to amount "intestate law" gives them if no Will is done. To avoid this issue most lawyers <u>use "disinterested" witnesses who aren't named in any gifts in the Will</u>. Though not required most lawyers try to not use witnesses named in Will to be Executor or be a Guardian. Often used as a witness is a friend, employee at some office or business, stranger, or family.

TESTATOR AND 2 WITNESSES USUALLY SIGN WILL AT A MEETING
To complete a Will the Testator signs and then 2 witnesses sign usually within minutes at a meeting. Everyone should be in 1 room and see hand of all signing. Witnesses just quietly read the 1 paragraph they sign and not whole Will. Witnesses showing ID is not required but usual. Testator initialing each Will page is not required. A Testator or a witness need not use their full legal name if they dislike it and rarely used it.

TESTATOR NEEDN'T DO OR SAY MORE EXCEPT SIGN
Some states but not Indiana require Testator say aloud it is their Will, which is called "publishing" a Will. Some Testators choose to chat and mention Will to witnesses to help show they know what they are doing.

MOST WILLS HAVE "MISCELLANEOUS" PART WITH HELPFUL LANGUAGE
Most Wills have "Miscellaneous" part of many paragraphs of legal language to avoid certain problems.

KEEP SIGNED WILL IN SAFE PLACE IT CAN BE FOUND AFTER A DEATH
People should keep a Will so it can be found within days of a death, like in desk, drawer, safe, or less often a safe deposit box. A Will can be given to someone to hold. It may help to tell someone where to find Will and any key. A Will can be filed at the local Circuit Court during a person's life for safekeeping but few people do this, and if filed and new Will is done usually people to avoid confusion withdraw the old filed Will.

CANCELING OLD WILLS IS USUALLY NOT A PROBLEM
So a new Will is followed old Wills should be canceled ("revoked") but this is easy and rarely a problem. A new Will can say old Wills are revoked to cancel them, and most do this including Will forms in this book. Also to revoke Will a person can write "void" or "cancelled" or "X" on a Will, preferably with a witness to it. In Indiana putting Will in garbage or people later not finding a Will may not be sufficient proof of revocation. Crossing out parts of Will often has no effect, and revoking a Will doesn't bring back earlier Wills.

MOST WILLS SAY USE LESS COSTLY AND SHORTER "INFORMAL" PROBATE
To help most Wills also say "use informal probate" which reduces some costs and delays. Usually the probate process to do things after a death is not too bad. Often over 95% of value gets to wanted persons.

MOST WILLS SAY TO SKIP COSTLY EXECUTOR OR GUARDIAN "BOND"
Most Wills helpfully say no "bond" or "surety" is required for an Executor, Guardian, or similar person. This is insurance bought from an insurance company to insure against misconduct. But the person doing a Will usually does not want this since any person named is trusted and insurance cost uses up estate assets.

WILL NAMES AN EXECUTOR TO DO THINGS AFTER A DEATH

WILL OFTEN NAMES "EXECUTOR" TO ACT AND HAVE POWER AFTER A DEATH
Often a Will names someone as "Executor" to act after a death like carry out gifts, handle debts, and do probate. The law gives Executors many powers and rights to do things, like collect and move money and property to new owners. If a Will does not name a person a judge picks someone, but close family may argue about who to pick. Naming 2 people to both do this job is possible but rare due to risk of arguments and delay, and since any 1 person named should be trusted. The person named Executor can get Will gifts.

"PERSONAL REPRESENTATIVE" IS NEW NAME FOR EXECUTOR
The term "Personal Representative" is now used in Wills and official legal papers for person handling things after a death like probate and estate, but people and this book still mostly use the old term Executor.

EXECUTOR CAN BE PAID AND ESTATE PAYS FOR THINGS
Many states let Executor ask for pay for hours worked or up to 5% of value of the estate (after debts), and this is often fair and minor. But pay is often not asked for to avoid income tax to Executor and leave more for Will gifts. Money an Executor needs like for fees, attorneys, or repairs comes from estate assets.

EXECUTOR CAN BE ANYONE AT LEAST 18 OFTEN LOCAL WITHOUT FELONY
An Executor must be 18 or older. They need not reside in Indiana but this may increase costs since an insurance bond may be required. A person with a felony criminal record can't be Executor. A lawyer or bank can be Executor but this is costly and they must agree. A judge can remove person doing a bad job. Some Wills add a second person to be Executor if first person is unavailable, but most Wills and people skip this since it is rarely needed and people know a judge can pick someone. If wanted, to add a second person to be Executor just add words like, "or if they are reasonably unable to serve I name _____ to serve".

CHAPTER 4
WILL GIFTS INCLUDING RESIDUE

MAIN USE OF WILL IS TO SAY GIFTS TO HAPPEN AFTER DEATH
Most people use Will to say what happens to their property and money after their death, usually by making various gifts in the Will. Verbal or even most written statements about this are not usually valid outside a Will. A Will can control property acquired after it was signed. Note, some families if all agree may try to informally hand out small items in way decedent said they wanted to gift, but this is not fully proper.

GIFTING IN WILL USING SIMPLE WORDS OFTEN IS BEST
Making gifts in a Will using simple words is often best, using words like "I give to" and "I gift to". This is legally fine and avoids confusing legal words like "bequest", "devise", and "legacy" which few people know.

PERSON IS MOSTLY FREE TO GIFT THEIR THINGS AS WANTED
People are mostly free to give at death their money and property as they want, like give a child nothing, give all to a charity, or give all to a distant friend. This book later explains some rights a spouse may have.

IN WILL CAN DO "SPECIFIC GIFTS" TO GIFT PARTICULAR PROPERTY
Most Wills have "specific gifts" to gift <u>particular things</u>. Specific gifts can be any property, like "I give boat to Ed Blom" and "I give UBank account #845534873 to Sue Wu". If a gift is not clear the law assumes all of a kind of thing is given, like "I give jewelry to Ann Po" means <u>all</u> jewelry. But giving specific property can have surprises like value of an item can greatly change or a Will gift may fail if property is no longer owned.

IN WILL CAN DO "GENERAL GIFTS" LIKE OF MONEY
Wills can do "general gifts" where what is gifted is not particular property but can be flexibly chosen, like "I give 1 of my 3 cars to Ed Po" which lets an Executor pick which car. The usual general gift is money, like "I give $5 to Ed Vu". Money gifts are easy to write, let equal gifts be made, and are safer since specific items might not be owned at death. To carry out money gifts an Executor uses accounts or sells some property.

"RESIDUE CLAUSE" IS CATCH-ALL THAT HELPFULLY GIFTS ANYTHING LEFT
Most Wills by their end have a Residue Clause to gift property or money not gifted or used in Will or other way, sometimes called a "catch-all" or "left-over" clause. <u>The Residue Clause is covered later in this Chapter.</u>

INDIANA ALLOWS "GIFT LISTS" TO BE DONE TO MAKE SOME GIFTS
As this book explains Indiana lets "Gift Lists" do some gifts of tangible personal property outside a Will.

PERSON IN WILL GIFT USUALLY MUST SURVIVE OR GIFT DOES NOT OCCUR
Many Wills like this book's Will forms say person named in Will gift must survive (live past) Testator for a gift to occur unless gift language specifically says otherwise. If survival is not clearly required for a Will gift what then occurs if a named recipient is dead can be unclear like due to confusing state "anti-lapse" laws. <u>People doing a Will should consider how Will gifts to people dying before Testator usually have no effect.</u> Many people if they see person in Will gift has died just re-do Will (or trust Residue Clause to handle gift).

SOME PEOPLE ADD "ALTERNATE BENEFICIARY" MAYBE FOR SPECIAL ITEMS

A person named in a Will gift dying before Testator is rare, and if seen most people just re-do Will to add new person or let Residue Clause handle it. But some people to prepare for this rare event maybe for special items write in an alternate beneficiary, like "I give Boat to Ed Wu but if they don't survive to Ben Fox".

WILL CAN SAY IF RECIPIENT DIES GIFT GOES TO "LINEAL DESCENDANTS"

A Will gift may say a gift goes to person but if they don't survive to their "lineal descendants per stirpes". Descendants are a person's children and grandchildren. "Per stirpes" is about "how" to spread things and means "by root" or "by branch", and basically tries to divide things so each family branch gets equal share. A family branch that died off with no one left is ignored. Most Wills use "lineal descendants" language in a Residue Clause and it also can be put in other gifts if wanted. An example shows how it works:

A Will may say **"Residue to Sue Wu but if they don't survive to lineal descendants per stirpes"**, and this means if Sue Wu died and a son Ken Wu is living and a son Ben Wu has died but left 2 children then Ken Wu gets 50% and Ben's 2 children each get 25%.

PROPERTY OR MONEY IN A JOINT GIFT GOES TO MULTIPLE PEOPLE

The same property or money in a "joint gift" can go to multiple people to each get a part interest, like "I give boat and all hats to Ann Wu and Sue Han" means each person owns 50% of every item. People later can split things by agreement or as Executor suggests, or Executor can sell items and split the money. If a person in a joint gift has died their part of things usually is left to transfer under the Residue Clause.

GIFT BENEFICIARIES CAN GET PERCENTAGE RATHER THAN EQUAL SHARE

If a Will gift goes to many people the law assumes equal shares, but if wanted percentages can be put, like "I give boat 91% to Ed Wu and 9% to Joe Hud". Often a Will Residue Clause uses percentages.

CONDITIONS ON WILL GIFTS ARE RARE DUE TO POSSIBLE PROBLEMS

Putting conditions on a gift, like "I give Ann Hud $90 if she graduates college", can cause problems like years of delay, risk of lawsuits, and big attorneys fees, and due to this conditions are rarely put on Will gifts.

HELPFUL LAWS OFTEN REQUIRE PERSON SURVIVE 120 HOURS TO GET GIFT

Laws in most states say person dying within 120 hours of someone is seen as having died earlier so often a Will gift to them is ignored. This avoids legal problems like need to know time of death if people die near each other, and avoids an item going to someone who quickly dies so item must be transferred again.

LATER DIVORCE OR MURDER CANCELS WILL GIFTS

Indiana law says a person divorcing or murdering Testator usually cancels any Will gifts to the person.

CAN LEAVE SOME WILL GIFT LINES BLANK OR WRITE THINGS LIKE "SKIPPED"

A person writing a Will can choose to not use some gifts lines in a Will legal form, like by just leaving them blank, writing things like "SKIPPED" or "NONE" in them, or using a computer to delete gift lines. Judges and others do not care about neatness or empty spaces in Wills.

RESIDUE CLAUSE GIFTING ALL LEFT IS MAIN WAY USED TO GIFT THINGS

THE "RESIDUE CLAUSE" IS CATCH-ALL THAT HELPS GIFT ANYTHING LEFT

Wills by their end have a Residue Clause to gift property or money not gifted earlier in Will or used in other ways. All things that transfers this way is called the "Residue". Many people gift most their money and property this way as it skips need to describe things and has less legal risk. Later after a death after applying a Residue Clause if anything is left (which happens in rare cases) then closest "heirs" get things (this means closest family). The Residue can go to multiple people and to avoid an equal split percentages can be used.

USUAL RESIDUE CLAUSE HAS 2 PARTS

A short 2 part Residue Clause is usual and is used in this book's Wills, and it has:

1) 1st space to name 1 or more persons to get things if they survive Testator (many name a spouse or closest family here), and if several people are named but only some survive then survivors get things, and

2) 2nd space to name persons to get things if all in 1st space don't survive (so these are fallbacks) (many name next family or friends here), and if a person in 2nd space died their descendants get their share.

EXAMPLE OF 2 PART RESIDUE CLAUSE:

"RESIDUE CLAUSE: I give money and property not gifted earlier:
A) to _____my husband John Paul Doe_____ if they survive me, then
B) to _____Sam Doe my son, Beth Wu my daughter, and Greta Fisher my friend_____ and if any of those just named do not survive me their part goes to their lineal descendants, per stirpes."

In this example if John Paul Doe has survived then he gets things. But if John Paul Doe hasn't survived and also Sam Doe hasn't survived and he left 2 daughters, then those 2 daughters split the 1/3 share of Sam Doe so get 1/6 each and other 2 persons in second part Beth Wu and Greta Fisher get 1/3 each.

A FEW PEOPLE RE-WRITE RESIDUE CLAUSE TO HAVE 1 PART

A normal Residue Clause of 2 parts is often fine and basically person put in 1st part usually gets things. A small fraction of people may want to modify a Will to have a "1 Part Residue Clause" which gifts to a group more equally, and also says if anyone named here die their descendants like children get their part. People with no spouse and no children are likelier to do this change, but even they often don't bother and just use this book's Will forms as is. See Example below for exact words to use if people want this change.

EXAMPLE OF 1 PART RESIDUE CLAUSE:

"RESIDUE CLAUSE: The rest, residue, and remainder of my estate, property of any kind and nature, and anything I have an interest in, I give to _Adam Doe and Beth Wu_ who survive me, and to lineal descendants per stirpes of any person just named who did not survive me."

In this example if Adam hasn't survived but had 2 children they each get 25%, and if Beth Wu survived she gets 50%. Or if Beth Wu also hadn't survived and had 5 kids they split her part and each gets 10%.

MUST SUFFICIENTLY DESCRIBE NAMES AND PROPERTY IN WILL GIFTS

WILL GIFT IS FINE IF CAN TELL WHAT TESTATOR LIKELY MEANT

The basic legal idea is a Will gift is sufficiently detailed if people who knew Testator can inform Executor or a judge what Testator meant more likely than not, and certainly is not needed to carry out a Will gift.

PUTTING NAMES OF PEOPLE OR GROUPS IN WILL GIFTS IS FAIRLY EASY

Names in Wills just must be enough so people who knew a Testator can say what likely was meant. It is assumed a person gifts to those they know so it's OK to use common names and nicknames unless 2 friends or family have the same name. Details can be added if Executor and family won't recognize a name or to be friendly, like "I give $5 to barber Ed Ax" and "I give $5 to my great kids Don Blom and Ann Rex". Names can be skipped if it won't cause confusion, like "I give $5 to each of my aunts". If a person mostly used a nickname "also known as" or "a/k/a" can be used to help, like "I give $5 to Ed Lee a/k/a Lucky Lee". A charity, group, or government can get a Will gift as long as they are not totally unofficial. Examples of descriptions of these in Will gifts are "I give $10 to Hart Food Shelf in Ivy, IN", "I give $5 to Gary city library", and "I give all stocks to Butler University in Indiana". People often just phone to ask for name of a charity.

DESCRIPTIONS OF PROPERTY IN WILL GIFTS IS FAIRLY EASY

Describing items in gifts is easy since people rarely own similar items, so often fine is "I give ax to Ed Wu" and "I give oak table to Sue Poe". It's OK to gift by category or list (like "I give tools to Ed Hart" and "I give laptop, flute, and horse to Ann Vix"). Financial assets can use plain words, like "bank accounts" or "stocks", but details can help, like "UBank account ending #1511". Using item location in a Will gift is risky as judges may ignore gift if it seems items were placed to affect gifting and not "independently significant" life reason. For example, "I give stuff in wall safe" or ""I give items in desk drawer" seems items were put places not for life reasons so judge may ignore this - but "I give bedroom tables" and "I give hats at cabin" probably is fine.

DESCRIBING REAL ESTATE IS HARD SO MANY USE RESIDUE OR TITLE

Real property can be gifted by street address or plain words, like "I give 28 Ivy Road, Hud, IN to Sue Ax" and "I give cabin in Lee County, IN to Ed Po". Such gifts do by law usually give all buildings and fixtures there and nearby land not separated by roads, but not other land. A "legal description" is best but hard to do right (like "Lot 3, Block 11 of Po's Addition to Hud City according to plat in land office in Ax County, Indiana". To make gifts of real property easy many use a Residue Clause for this, or just add people on title to land.

SIMPLE WILL WITH MOST GIFTING DONE BY RESIDUE CLAUSE IS OFTEN BEST

Writing a simple Will without many gifts and much left blank and then using Residue Clause is often best.

If there is a spouse often people do a few small gifts to friends and other family, then use Residue Clause of Will to gift spouse the Residue, and then name a few fallback persons in the Residue Clause.

If there is no spouse often people do a few small gifts, then name family or friends to get the Residue.

A parent with young children if married to other parent often gifts Residue to them, and as fallback gifts the Residue to the children. Or if not married a parent mostly gifts to their children using the Residue Clause.

CHAPTER 5
DEBT, MARRIAGE, AND YOUNG CHILD ISSUES

DEBT, MARRIAGE, AND YOUNG CHILD CAN CAUSE ISSUES
This Chapter deals with <u>debt issues</u>, <u>marriage issues</u>, and <u>young child issues</u>. People can skip the parts of this Chapter they think won't matter to them.

DEBT ISSUES

PAYING DECEDENT'S DEBTS MAY USE UP RESOURCES AND REDUCE GIFTS
Creditors decedent owed can ask judge to be paid from decedent's money and property before Will gifts and other transfers are done. But if decedent had under about $50,000 of money and property plus a house creditors often don't bother, for reasons said below. Resources to pay debts first come from things in Will Residue, then Will general gifts like of money, then Will specific gifts, and then any non-probate transfers. Some debts like for probate, attorney, funeral, and health care have priority to be paid first. Helpfully spouse and family aren't usually personally liable to pay decedent's debts unless they guaranteed or co-signed. <u>People should consider how paying debts may use up money or property, leaving less to carry out Will gifts</u>.

BEFORE DEBTS ARE PAID MAY COME SOME FAMILY RIGHTS
Most states say surviving spouse and children can claim "family rights" before debts are paid to let family get something despite big debts. Many states give family a 1) "living allowance" right to claim money to live on a year, 2) "exempt property" right to often $30,000 of decedent's personal property, and 3) "homestead" right explained later. Creditors know of family rights so often don't seek payment if told decedent left little. <u>Often a person by Will gifts mostly to family like over 50% so they're happy and don't bother to claim family rights</u>, but if family rights are used it may leave little to carry out Will gifts. People can research their state.

"HOMESTEAD" LAWS IN SOME STATES PROTECT HOME FOR FAMILY
"Homestead" laws in many states say decedent's creditors can't seek payment by foreclosing and then selling decedent's house if spouse or children under 18 are there (unless equity is big, like over $100,000). Homestead laws also often say spouse or minor children get ownership of decedent's house (or right to live there for their life in some states) if decedent owned it and despite a Will gift giving it to other people. <u>Often a person gives house to family by Will or by putting them on title so they are happy and don't bother with these rights</u>, but if rights are used it may interfere with Will gifts. People can research their state.

OFTEN SECURED DEBTS LIKE MORTGAGE OR VEHICLE LIEN AREN'T PAID OFF
Most states say secured debts like house mortgage or car lien are <u>not</u> paid off after death but remain even if Will says generally to pay debts. This book's Wills clearly say don't pay secured debts unless person writes in Will to do so. This avoids using up much money and property so little is left to carry out Will gifts. If a Testator wants to pay off secured debts a) they can in Will gift a person enough cash to pay them, or b) write order to pay in Will (like "I order mortgage on cabin paid off"). Of course people who get gift of car or house with a lien or mortgage must pay monthly payments to avoid later foreclosure or repossession.

MARRIAGE ISSUES

MOST STATES USE "SEPARATE PROPERTY LAW" FOR SPOUSES

Most states including Indiana use "Separate Property Law" system saying a married person mostly owns all their money and property separately and not jointly 50/50. Due to this a spouse is mostly free to sell during life their things, or gift in Will their things. But joint ownership by 2 spouses can arise by special ways (like by agreement, paying half a purchase price, and many spouses do paperwork to own a house jointly).

"COMMUNITY PROPERTY" LAW APPLIES IN OTHER STATES FOR SPOUSES

There are 9 states mostly in West and South U.S.A. that use "Community Property" law for spouses (Arizona, California, Louisiana, Idaho, Nevada, New Mexico, Texas, Washington, and also Wisconsin). This says if a married person lives in these states most property or money gotten is usually owned 50/50 by spouses as "Community Property" if it relates to activities during a marriage (like from labor or wages, or active management of a small business) or if bought or improved with existing Community Property. Most people avoid these issues unless recently moving to or from these states.

"JOINT WILL" SIGNED BY BOTH SPOUSES IS NOT RECOMMENDED

Some couples sign 1 "Joint Will" or "Contract To Make A Will" done by lawyer which says spouses gives all to the other if they die first, then says last living spouse gives to all children equally, and usually says a spouse may not change this. This is not recommended, banned in some states, and few people do this.

SPOUSE CAN SEEK "ELECTIVE SHARE" FOR SHARE OF DECEDENT'S THINGS

For fairness and to ensure surviving spouse has enough to live on, many states give spouse if unhappy with what Will gifts them a right to choose (elect) an "Elective Share" of their spouse's property and money. This avoids spouse feeling to be safe they must divorce and get property or money rather than stay married. Indiana sets the Elective Share at 1/2, or a bit less if the deceased was married before and left children from a different marriage. Some other states use a percentage that increases to 50% with years of marriage. A spouse who abandons a marriage for no good reason for years may lose Elective Share rights, but to be safe some people divorce. To avoid legal tricks an Elective Share may cover items a spouse gave away recently or controlled but didn't officially own. An unhappy spouse might also sue for promises, like "He said I get fair share and house if I stayed while he was sick and did work". Due to all this a married person often gifts by Will and other ways mostly to a spouse (like 50% and the house). People can research their state.

YOUNG CHILD ISSUES

WILL CAN NAME "GUARDIAN OF THE PERSON" TO CARE FOR CHILD

If a parent dies with child under 18 the other natural or adopted parent (but not step-parent) automatically then takes over daily care and control of home, school, and health care unless the parent is unavailable or proven unfit in court which is rare. But just in case it is needed a Will can name someone as "Guardian of the Person" to do these things involving caring for a child. Since naming other parent is pointless (they take over if fit and available) most Wills name as Guardian of the Person a healthy friend or relative just in case

this is ever needed. Wishes for this of last living parent has more weight. If no Will names person the family can ask judge to do this, but family may argue about this. Naming 2 persons to both serve is rare since these 2 may argue and any 1 person named is usually trusted, but some people name a married couple.

WILL CAN NAME "GUARDIAN OF THE ESTATE" TO MANAGE ASSETS OF CHILD

A child until 18 legally can't easily manage money or property, so in a Will a person can be named as "Guardian of the Estate" to help in case child gets any assets. They manage money and property of child and pick what to pay of minor's school, health care, and living costs till 18 when all left usually goes to child. By law money and property **must** be spent only on child. Since often 1 parent will be still alive <u>most people in Will name other parent as Guardian of the Estate</u> because they'll know what spending is best and may argue with others, but a different person can be named if other parent is super unreliable or bad with money. If no Will names a person or they're unavailable to serve (which is rare) close family can have judge pick person, but family may argue about this. Naming 2 persons to both serve is rare as the 2 may argue and the 1 person named is trusted, but some name a married couple. People paying for home or necessities for a child including a Guardian can ask to be paid back from child's money and property. Judges often hold a helpful yearly hearing looking for misuse of money or property. <u>Note, it is fine to keep it simple and pick the same 1 person as both kinds of Guardians</u> to handle all things for a child if this is ever needed.

TO HELP CHILD MUST BE 18 AND ALTERNATE PERSON RARELY IS NEEDED

A person must be at least 18 to be a Guardian and usually they can't have a felony criminal record or record of child abuse. A Guardian need not be a Indiana resident or U.S. citizen, but being local may help with later work. Some Wills add a second person to serve if first person is unavailable, like by adding: "or if they are reasonably unable to serve I name _____ to serve". But this is rarely done since rarely is a person unavailable and if seen early a new Will is done or later a judge just picks a person.

NAMING PERSONS TO HELP CHILD RARELY MATTERS MUCH

Naming these people to help a child rarely matters, so parents shouldn't worry too much. A study shows just 0.2% of children under 19 had 2 parents die to leave a child parentless and likely to need much help. See <u>Socioeconomic Parent Mortality, Census Bureau 288</u>. It is also rare for a child to get property or money since other parent left to raise a family usually gets everything. A judge also has power to act to help a child.

WILLS SAY "CUSTODIAN" CAN HOLD AND SPEND MINOR'S THINGS ON THEM

Often a Will helpfully says Executor may choose <u>to have "Custodian" get things for minor under age 18 using the "Uniform Transfers To Minor Act" law</u>, to hold money and property of minor under 18, decide how to spend things on minor, and then anything of value left goes to minor at 18 or age picked from 18 to 25. This law was done in 1990s <u>to mostly fix all problems people had about costs, attorneys' fees, time, work, and paperwork caused by normal Guardians and Trusts</u>. This book's Will forms in the final full paragraph says the person named in Will as Guardian of the Estate or if they can't serve the person named in Will as Executor may be "Custodian" and hold and spend a minor's property and money till 18.

CHAPTER 6
BASIC IDEAS ABOUT HEALTH CARE FORMS

SOME BASIC IDEAS HELP USE HEALTH CARE FORMS

■ By law people control their health care unless "incapacitated" by inability to a) <u>communicate</u> verbally or by notes, b) be <u>rational</u>, or c) be <u>conscious.</u> Unless totally incapacitated people just tell doctor their wishes. Most people keep control of health care till death or till no big options remain, but <u>people worry so do health care forms which mostly only matter if person is incapacitated</u>.

■ Parents <u>do</u> have power over health care of <u>child under 18</u>. If an <u>older person becomes incapacitated the closest family like spouse or adult child can make emergency decisions</u> but they usually must then rush to a judge to get further power if no form names them Agent for health care.

■ In forms a person can <u>name an "Agent"</u> to take control later if needed or help make decisions, and naming an Agent (often spouse or adult child) can avoid family later having to rush to get power from judge.

■ In forms people can give <u>written instructions doctors, family, and any Agent must obey</u>, but many skip this as hard to write and it may legal issues and delay. People can give instructions but skip naming an Agent.

■ **Young people** often skip health care forms since they rarely are very ill. But some **married people** do a form to name spouse as Agent. **People 19-25** sometimes do a form just to name parents as Agents.

■ **Older people** over 40 often do form naming Agent but many skip instructions to not limit the freedom of their Agent, but people with strong wishes might write instructions carefully maybe with a doctor's help.

■ <u>Most people do fairly long health care form</u> with spot to name an Agent just in case this is needed, and spot for instructions. Names for the form vary. Other forms are usually only done by oldest or sickest people

■ Pain relief like pain drugs and comfort care is usually given even if forms say to stop or limit other care.

■ For <u>rare cases stopping health care ("pulling plug") may be issue</u> due to sick person being a) incapacitated so unable to control things, and b) in bad health with poor quality of life and little chance of recovery:

-- most people <u>do nothing special and trust family or Agent to decide on stopping care</u> based on changing complex factors like pain, cost, hassle, suffering and time of treatment, beliefs, and chances of recovery;

-- a few people do a serious legal document or just write in more plain document <u>to block health care</u> if **later** doctors see person has irrevocable terminal condition and <u>see further medical care likely won't help</u> (this action is <u>often called doing a **"Living Will"**</u> even if the form used is not titled this);

-- a few people do a serious legal document to **starting immediately** block health care listed, often called "Do-Not-Resuscitate" if short and only about C.P.R., or often called "Physician's Order" if covering more.

CHAPTER 7
FORM 1: LAST WILL AND TESTAMENT (STANDARD)

FORM 1 IS A STANDARD WILL THAT IS FLEXIBLE WITH NO GUARDIANS

Form 1 is a standard Will that is flexible and is the Will form most people use. It has no part about Guardians so is usually for person with no child under age 18.

FORM 1 IS WILL WITH SEVERAL PARTS

Will at start has place for person doing Will (Testator) to write their <u>full legal name</u> unless they dislike it and rarely used it, and write county of residence at the time (a Will is still valid if people move later).

The 1st paragraph, "Gifts", has many spaces to make either specific gifts of particular property or general gifts like of money. People can delete, copy and paste to add more, or leave blank these gift lines.

The 2nd paragraph, says to follow any separate writings done apart from the Will that gifts tangible personal property in way allowed by law.

The 3rd paragraph, "Residue", has a Residue Clause to say any property and money left after other Will parts and any other transfers is gifted to persons as the Residue Clause directs.

The 4th paragraph, "Administration", has space to name an Executor to handle legal and other matters after death, but the newer term "Personal Representative" is used here for this.

The 5th paragraph, "Miscellaneous", has sentences of legal language to help avoid certain legal issues.

Last is paragraph for person doing Will to sign, and paragraph for 2 witnesses to sign and put addresses.

USUAL RESIDUE CLAUSE HAS 2 PLACES TO NAME PERSONS TO GET THINGS

In a Will "Residue Clause" anything left after other Will parts is transferred as the clause directs. Many people use Residue Clause to gift most or even all things. In this Will form's Residue Clause there is:
1) a 1st space to name 1 or more persons to get the Residue, and if any named here have not survived and died before the Will maker then any other persons named here take their share,
2) a 2nd space to name people to get things if all in 1st space died before Will maker, and if any people named here didn't survive their shares go to "lineal descendants" like their children.

Most people name in 1st space a spouse or closest family or closest friends, and in 2nd space next closest family or friends. This may seem complicated but usually those in 1st area of Residue Clause get things.

TESTATOR AND 2 WITNESSES WHILE TOGETHER SIGN WILL

A Will after being filled out (except bits intentionally left blank) then usually should be signed by the Testator doing the Will in front of 2 witnesses who sign too. Testator can be silent and do nothing but sign, but often they chat and mention the Will to help show they are acting voluntarily and are of sound mind. It is best to use witnesses at least age 18, not getting gifts in Will, and not named Executor or Guardian in the Will. Having witnesses show people ID and giving contact information is not required but often done. When signing the Testator and 2 witnesses should be in same room and see each other as they sign. Witnesses usually before signing silently read the 1 paragraph they sign and not the entire Will.

LAST WILL AND TESTAMENT

I, _____, of _____ County, Indiana, do revoke all prior Wills, Testaments, and Codicils, and do make, publish, and declare this to be my Will. When doing this I am of sound mind and under no duress or undue influence.

1. GIFTS. I give these gifts in this Will, but to get a gift in this section the recipient must survive me except as otherwise stated below.

I give _____ to _____.

I give _____ to _____.

I give _____ to _____.

I give _____ to _____.

I give _____ to _____.

I give _____ to _____.

I give _____ to _____.

I give _____ to _____.

I give _____ to _____.

I give _____ to _____.

I give _____ to _____.

I give _____ to _____.

2. GIFTS OF TANGIBLE PERSONAL PROPERTY BY SEPARATE WRITINGS. I may gift tangible personal property by writings separate from a Will. Such a writing not found within 90 days of my death is canceled and of no effect. Such a writing existing when this Will is done is not revoked or canceled unless this Will specifically says this.

3. RESIDUE. I give the rest and residue and remainder of my estate, my money and property of any kind and nature, and anything I have an interest in so long as it was not transferred by other Will provisions (all of which is called the "residue"), as follows:
   a) to _____ who survive me with persons just named who survive me taking the share of non-survivors, then
   b) to _____ and if any of those just named do not survive me their part goes to their lineal descendants per stirpes.

4. ADMINISTRATION. I name and appoint _____ as Personal Representative including for me, my Will, and my estate.

5. MISCELLANEOUS. The following applies to this Will and generally.
   Priority of Will gifts of the same type is based on the order they are written.
   In this document no unfilled part is a mistake and residue spaces may be left blank.
   The words "give" and "gift" also means a devise, bequest, grant, legacy, or similar.
   A gift of property no longer owned by Testator at death shall lapse and be of no effect including no payment of money shall be done in its place, all without ademption.
   If gift or gift section mentions survival, survive, or surviving then survival is an absolute condition and anti-lapse laws or similar have no effect.
   Any failure to make gifts to family including children is intentional and not a mistake.
   No gift or transfer made during life reduces or offsets a Will gift unless during my life I expressly usually called it a "loan" or "advancement".
   Use of particular gender shall include other genders, reference to singular or plural shall be interchangeable, and "they" may be singular or plural.
   Unless parts of this Will specifically says otherwise a secured debt like mortgage or lien on real property or vehicles shall not be paid off, recipient of property takes it subject to liens, and no recipient who has debtor take property or get payment via use or threat of a secured debt may require a devisee, recipient, heir, or estate to pay or do anything.
   I give any Personal Representative a) the fullest authority, powers, and discretion allowed by state law, b) authority to lease, sell, mortgage, convey, or retain property including real property in any such manner and time they deem helpful or proper, and c) authority to anytime pay or settle claims or debts if they in their sole discretion chooses.
   Any Personal Representative shall not be required to render and file annual or other accountings with respect to property or money including in relation to my Will or estate. Any Personal Representative may act independently in all ways without supervision.

I request informal or administrative probate of my Will and estate without supervision.

If context permits the terms Personal Representative, Executor, and Administrator shall be seen as interchangeable as if all were written, and if context permits the term Guardian of the Estate is interchangeable with Guardian of Property and Conservator.

The residue includes lapsed or failed gifts, insurance paid to estate, inheritances owed me, and property I had a power of appointment or testamentary disposition over.

Any Personal Representative, Executor, Guardian of any kind, Conservator, and any fiduciary under this Will or otherwise, shall qualify and serve without bond, security, surety, or similar, including despite place of residence or lack of ties to a state or country.

A Guardian of any kind should serve all persons without full capacity in my care.

This Will does not revoke a Living Will or any legal document concerning health care.

A Personal Representative using their sole discretion has power at any time to transfer a minor child's money or property to person named Guardian of the Estate in Will to serve as Custodian under the Indiana Uniform Transfers to Minors Act or similar law here or in other states, to serve until minor is 18, all without bond our any court action. If they are unable to serve the person named Personal Representative in Will shall be Custodian.

TESTATOR

IN WITNESS WHEREOF, I, the Testator doing this Will, do now sign, declare, and publish this document as my Will, this ___ day of _____, 20___.

_____
Testator signature

WITNESSES

We, the Witnesses who are named below, say the Testator named above did sign, declare, and publish this document as the Testator's Will when he appeared to be of sound mind and acting voluntarily and not under duress, and we the Witnesses in Testator's presence and presence of each other have hereunto signed our names acting as witnesses on the ___ day of _____, 20___.

_____   _____
Witness signature   Witness address

_____   _____
Witness signature   Witness address

CHAPTER 8
FORM 2: LAST WILL AND TESTAMENT (GUARDIANS)

FORM 2 IS BASIC WILL WITH GUARDIANS CLAUSE FOR THOSE NEEDING THIS
Form 2 is a Will with Guardians clause for people with child under 18 or caring for incapacitated person.

FORM HAS SEVERAL PARTS
Will at start has place for person doing Will (Testator) to write their <u>full legal name</u> unless they dislike it and rarely used it, and write county of residence at the time (a Will is still valid if people move later).

The 1st paragraph, "Gifts", has many spaces to make either specific gifts of particular property or general gifts like of money. People can delete, copy and paste to add more, or leave blank these gift lines.

The 2nd paragraph, says to follow any separate writings done apart from the Will that gifts tangible personal property in way allowed by law.

The 3rd paragraph, "Residue", has a Residue Clause to say any property and money left after other Will parts and any other transfers is gifted to persons as the Residue Clause directs.

The 4th paragraph, "Administration", has space to name an Executor to handle legal and other matters after death, but the newer term "Personal Representative" is used here for this.

<u>The 5th paragraph, "Guardians", lets "Guardian of the Person" be named to care for child if needed, and lets "Guardian of the Estate" be named to manage a child's property and money if needed</u>.

The 6th paragraph, "Miscellaneous", has sentences of legal language to help avoid certain legal issues.

Last is paragraph for person doing Will to sign, and paragraph for 2 witnesses to sign and put addresses.

USUAL RESIDUE CLAUSE HAS 2 PLACES TO NAME PERSONS TO GET THINGS
In a Will "Residue Clause" anything left after other Will parts is transferred as the clause directs. Many people use Residue Clause to gift most or even all things. In this Will form's Residue Clause there is:
1) a 1st space to name 1 or more persons to get the Residue, and if any named here have not survived and died before the Will maker then any other persons named here take their share,
2) a 2nd space to name people to get things if all in 1st space died before Will maker, and if any people named here didn't survive their shares go to "lineal descendants" like their children.

Most people name in 1st space a spouse or closest family or closest friends, and in 2nd space next closest family or friends. This may seem complicated but usually those in 1st area of Residue Clause get things.

TESTATOR AND 2 WITNESSES WHILE TOGETHER SIGN WILL
A Will after being filled out (except bits intentionally left blank) then usually should be signed by the Testator doing the Will in front of 2 witnesses who sign too. Testator can be silent and do nothing but sign, but often they chat and mention the Will to help show they are acting voluntarily and are of sound mind. It is best to use witnesses at least age 18, not getting gifts in Will, and not named Executor or Guardian in the Will. Having witnesses show people ID and giving contact information is not required but often done. When signing the Testator and 2 witnesses should be in same room and see each other as they sign. Witnesses usually before signing silently read the 1 paragraph they sign and not the entire Will.

LAST WILL AND TESTAMENT

I, _____, of _____ County, Indiana, do revoke all prior Wills, Testaments, and Codicils, and do make, publish, and declare this to be my Will. When doing this I am of sound mind and under no duress or undue influence.

1. GIFTS. I give these gifts in this Will, but to get a gift in this section the recipient must survive me except as otherwise stated below.

I give _____ to _____.

I give _____ to _____.

I give _____ to _____.

I give _____ to _____.

I give _____ to _____.

I give _____ to _____.

I give _____ to _____.

I give _____ to _____.

I give _____ to _____.

I give _____ to _____.

I give _____ to _____.

I give _____ to _____.

2. GIFTS OF TANGIBLE PERSONAL PROPERTY BY SEPARATE WRITINGS. I may gift tangible personal property by writings separate from a Will. Such a writing not found within 90 days of my death is canceled and of no effect. Such a writing existing when this Will is done is not revoked or canceled unless this Will specifically says this.

3. RESIDUE. I give the rest and residue and remainder of my estate, my money and property of any kind and nature, and anything I have an interest in so long as it was not transferred by other Will provisions (all of which is called the "residue"), as follows:

   a) to _____ who survive me with persons just named who survive me taking the share of non-survivors, then

   b) to _____ and if any of those just named do not survive me their part goes to their lineal descendants per stirpes.

4. ADMINISTRATION. I name and appoint _____ as Personal Representative including for me, my Will, and my estate.

5. GUARDIANS. I name and appoint _____ as Guardian of the Person to have care, custody, and control of the person of any minor child of mine. I also name and appoint _____ as Guardian of the Estate of any minor child of mine and their money, property, and estate.

6. MISCELLANEOUS. The following applies to this Will and generally.

   Priority of Will gifts of the same type is based on the order they are written.

   In this document no unfilled part is a mistake and residue spaces may be left blank.

   The words "give" and "gift" also means a devise, bequest, grant, legacy, or similar.

   A gift of property no longer owned by Testator at death shall lapse and be of no effect including no payment of money shall be done in its place, all without ademption.

   If gift or gift section mentions survival, survive, or surviving then survival is an absolute condition and anti-lapse laws or similar have no effect.

   Any failure to make gifts to family including children is intentional and not a mistake.

   No gift or transfer made during life reduces or offsets a Will gift unless during my life I expressly usually called it a "loan" or "advancement".

   Use of particular gender shall include other genders, reference to singular or plural shall be interchangeable, and "they" may be singular or plural.

   Unless parts of this Will specifically says otherwise a secured debt like mortgage or lien on real property or vehicles shall not be paid off, recipient of property takes it subject to liens, and no recipient who has debtor take property or get payment via use or threat of a secured debt may require a devisee, recipient, heir, or estate to pay or do anything.

   I give any Personal Representative a) the fullest authority, powers, and discretion allowed by state law, b) authority to lease, sell, mortgage, convey, or retain property including real property in any such manner and time they deem helpful or proper, and c) authority to anytime pay or settle claims or debts if they in their sole discretion chooses.

Any Personal Representative shall not be required to render and file annual or other accountings with respect to property or money including in relation to my Will or estate. Any Personal Representative may act independently in all ways without supervision.

I request informal or administrative probate of my Will and estate without supervision.

If context permits the terms Personal Representative, Executor, and Administrator shall be seen as interchangeable as if all were written, and if context permits the term Guardian of the Estate is interchangeable with Guardian of Property and Conservator.

The residue includes lapsed or failed gifts, insurance paid to estate, inheritances owed me, and property I had a power of appointment or testamentary disposition over.

Any Personal Representative, Executor, Guardian of any kind, Conservator, and any fiduciary under this Will or otherwise, shall qualify and serve without bond, security, surety, or similar, including despite place of residence or lack of ties to a state or country.

A Guardian of any kind should serve all persons without full capacity in my care.

This Will does not revoke a Living Will or any legal document concerning health care.

A Personal Representative using their sole discretion has power at any time to transfer a minor child's money or property to person named Guardian of the Estate in Will to serve as Custodian under the Indiana Uniform Transfers to Minors Act or similar law here or in other states, to serve until minor is 18, all without bond our any court action. If they are unable to serve the person named Personal Representative in Will shall be Custodian.

TESTATOR

IN WITNESS WHEREOF, I, the Testator doing this Will, do now sign, declare, and publish this document as my Will, this ___ day of _____, 20___ .

_____
Testator signature

WITNESSES

We, the Witnesses who are named below, say the Testator named above did sign, declare, and publish this document as the Testator's Will when he appeared to be of sound mind and acting voluntarily and not under duress, and we the Witnesses in Testator's presence and presence of each other have hereunto signed our names acting as witnesses on the __ day of _____, 20____ .

_____   _____
Witness signature   Witness address

_____   _____
Witness signature   Witness address

CHAPTER 9
FORM 3: SELF-PROVING CLAUSE

FORM CAN BE DONE TO SUPPORT A WILL
The Self-Proving Clause form can be done to help reduce later legal work, but this form is optional and is not needed to have a valid Will.

FORM SAVES LATER WORK OF SHOWING WILL WAS PROPERLY SIGNED
The Testator and 2 witnesses who signed a Will can also sign a Self-Proving Clause form, and this helps to later when trying to use a Will "prove" it was properly signed. If this form is not done after death work may be needed to get testimony of witnesses to the Will signing, someone familiar with signatures of people, or handwriting expert. If this form is not done there is bit more risk a Will is not followed.

INDIANA DOES NOT REQUIRE FORM BE SIGNED IN FRONT OF NOTARY
Many states have a similar "Self-Proving Affidavit" which helps prove a Will was properly signed but they require a notary see it signed. Indiana law is nice and does not require a notary for this kind of document. Since Indiana does not require a notary there is no reason to not do a Self-Proving Clause when Testator and Witnesses do Will. Some lawyers who write Wills combine Will signature page and Self-Proving Clause into 1 page but this can be confusing.

FORM IS DONE BY TESTATOR AND 2 WITNESSES SIGNING
For Self-Proving Clause to be completed a Testator and 2 witnesses just must date and sign the form. The form is often done within minutes of when Will is signed but it also can be done any time later too. Once done the Self-Proving Clause if often kept with the Will it supports.

SELF-PROVING CLAUSE

We, the undersigned Testator and the undersigned Witnesses, respectively, whose names are signed to the attached or foregoing instrument declare:

(1) that the Testator executed the instrument as the Testator's Will;

(2) that, in the presence of both Witnesses, the Testator signed or acknowledged the signature already made or directed another to sign for the Testator in the Testator's presence;

(3) that the Testator executed the Will as a free and voluntary act for the purposes expressed in it;

(4) that each of the Witnesses, in the presence of the Testator and of each other, signed the will as a Witness;

(5) that the Testator was of sound mind when the Will was executed; and

(6) that to the best knowledge of each of the Witnesses the Testator was, at the time the Will was executed, at least 18 years of age or was a member of the armed forces or of the merchant marine of the United States or its allies.

_____ _____
Date   Testator

                                                                         _____
                                                                         Witness

                                                                         _____
                                                                         Witness

CHAPTER 10
FORM 4: TANGIBLE PERSONAL PROPERTY LIST

FORM LETS GIFTS OF NORMAL PROPERTY BE EASILY MADE AFTER WILL

Form lets people after or before Will is done easily write more gifts of property to occur after their death, but as explained below this is limited to "tangible personal property".

FORM GIVES EASY QUICK WAY TO WRITE GIFTS

The form in this chapter, often just called the "List" form or less often a "Memo" form, lets person before or after Will has been done write more gifts of property to occur after death without hassle of doing new Will. For Lists to be used <u>a Will must say Lists can be used</u> and this book's Wills say this. This book's Will forms say any existing Lists are not revoked by the Will. If List and Will gift the same item then the Will is followed. People can do many Lists over time and all can count. If multiple Lists gift the same item the more recent List controls. People can change Lists by crossing out, erasing, or adding words, but people should put a new date and signature at bottom. To cut uncertainty this book's forms say a List not found within 90 days of death is ignored. People to cancel a List can rip it, mark it like "void" or "X", or just throw it away.

It may help to see the Indiana law allowing Lists, which says:

"**Ind. Code 29-1-6-1(m).**

A written statement or list that: (1) complies with this subsection; and (2) is referred to in a will; may be used to dispose of items of tangible personal property, other than property used in a trade or business, not otherwise specifically disposed of by the will.

To be admissible under this subsection as evidence of the intended disposition, the writing must be signed by the testator and must describe the items and the beneficiaries with reasonable certainty.

The writing may be prepared before or after the execution of the will.

The writing may be altered by the testator after the writing is prepared.

The writing may have no significance apart from the writing's effect on the dispositions made by the will.

If more than 1 otherwise effective writing exists, then, to the extent of a conflict among the writings, the provisions of the most recent writing revoke the inconsistent provisions of each earlier writing."

CAN ONLY GIFT "TANGIBLE PERSONAL PROPERTY"

The List form can gift only "tangible personal property" so tangible (touchable) things (not accounts or most investments) and not "real property" (land or buildings). It can't cover cash or coins even if antiques. It can't cover items used in a business including inventory. Improper property written in a form is ignored.

TO COMPLETE GIFT LIST SIGN AND DATE

To be valid a List form just must be signed and dated. If many pages of List forms are done they are usually kept together and paper-clipped to a Will.

TANGIBLE PERSONAL PROPERTY LIST

   In this writing are gifts to occur at my death of tangible personal property not specifically disposed of by my Will.

   A writing not found within 90 days of my death shall have no effect.

   I may do many pages of these writings at different times and they all should be seen as 1 document, and if any conflicts occur the more recently done page controls.

   If a person getting a gift below does not survive me such gift shall lapse and instead that property passes as my Will says including by Will residue clause.

PROPERTY ITEMS   **NAMES OF RECIPIENTS**

_____ to _____

_____ to _____

_____ to _____

_____ to _____

_____ to _____

_____ to _____

_____ to _____

_____ to _____

_____ to _____

_____ to _____

_____ to _____

_____ to _____

_____ to _____

_____ to _____

_____ to _____

DATE:_____   **SIGNED:**_____

CHAPTER 11
FORM 5: ADVANCE DIRECTIVE

FORM CAN NAME HEALTH CARE REPRESENTATIVE

This form lets person name someone as "Health Care Representative" to make health care decisions if person is later incapacitated. The form in this book is a popular form written by a group of hospitals and other health care organizations. <u>Many people do just this 1 form and skip other health care forms.</u>

CAN NAME "HEALTH CARE REPRESENTATIVE" TO HAVE POWER

Form lets "Health Care Representative" be named to get power to make medical decisions if person is ever incapacitated so can't control their healthcare themselves. Often named Representative is spouse, adult child, relative, or friend. Naming a family member can avoid need to rush to see judge to get power in an emergency. A person's doctor or anyone associated with a place giving health care can't be named as the Representative. There is a spot to name second person to serve if first person is unavailable but many people don't bother with this since this is rarely needed. <u>The form also has 3 boxes to pick 1 to put an X or check in, which lets person say if later very ill what are a person's wishes about stopping health care</u>.

PERSON SIGNS FORM IN FRONT OF NOTARY OR 2 WITNESSES

To complete form a person signs in front of notary or 2 witnesses at least 18 who then also sign form. Neither witness can be named as Health Care Representative in the form, and at last 1 witness can't be a relative or spouse of relative of the person doing the form. A person can keep the signed form until needed or immediately hand it to the Representative or family members to hold and use if needed. Usually the form should be shown to any place that may give care to make it part of a person's medical file. To cancel form a person should tell Representative and then usually tell any place shown the form it is canceled.

INDIANA ADVANCE DIRECTIVE

INDIANA HEALTH CARE REPRESENTATIVE:
A Health Care Representative is a person chosen by you to make healthcare decisions, including end-of-life decisions, if you are unable to make your own. It is a good idea to talk with this person about your preferences ahead of time. A doctor will determine if you are unable to make your own decisions.

My name (Full Legal Name – also known as "declarant")   Date of Birth (MM/DD/YYYY)

_____   _____

My Health Care Representative can make decisions for me if I cannot make and share my own health care decisions. My Health Care Representative must follow my wishes and values. My values include my ideas about dignity and quality of life. If my Health Care Representative does not know my wishes, my Health Care Representative must act in good faith and make decisions in my best interests. These decisions include but are not limited to:

- Agreeing to medical treatment
- Stopping medical treatment
- Refusing medical treatment
- Arranging comfort care

I want the following person to be my Health Care Representative (HCR):

HCR Name   HCR Phone Number

_____   _____

If my primary HCR named above is not able or available to act for me, I want the following person to be my backup Health Care Representative:

Backup HCR Name   Backup HCR Phone Number

_____   _____

OPTIONAL STATEMENT OF PREFERENCES:
I would like to provide some additional guidance for my Health Care Representative on my end of life preferences. (Please select only one option below).

☐ The ***quality of my life*** is more important than the length of my life. If I am unable to make my own decisions and my attending physician believes that I will not recover, I do not want treatments to prolong my life or delay my death. Instead, I would want treatment or care to make me comfortable and to relieve me of pain.

☐ ***Staying alive*** is more important to me, no matter how sick I am or how unlikely my chances for recovery are. I want my life to be prolonged to the greatest extent possible, in accordance with reasonable medical standards.

☐ I choose to NOT complete this section at this time.

Declarant Name: _____

REQUIRED SIGNATURES:
By signing this form, I cancel and revoke every health care power of attorney I signed in the past.

_____   _____
Signature (Declarant)   Date

_____
Printed Name (Declarant)

This form must be either signed by 2 adult witnesses (below left) or notarized (below right) to be legally valid.

SIGNATURE OF 2 ADULT WITNESSES	*NOTARIZATION*
Each of the undersigned Witnesses confirms that he or she has received satisfactory proof of the identity of the Declarant and is satisfied that the Declarant is of sound mind and has the capacity to sign the above Advance Directive. **At least one of the undersigned Witnesses is not a spouse or other relative of the Declarant.**	STATE OF INDIANA)) SS: COUNTY OF _____) Before me, a Notary Public, personally appeared _____ [*name of signing Declarant*], who acknowledged the execution of the foregoing Advance Directive as his or her voluntary act, and who, having been duly sworn, stated that any representations therein are true. Witness my hand and Notarial Seal on this _____ day of _____, 20____.
_____ Signature of Adult Witness 1	_____ Signature of Notary Public
_____ Printed Name of Adult Witness 1	_____ Notary's Printed Name *(if not on seal)*
_____ Date	_____ Commission Number *(if not on seal)*
_____ Signature of Adult Witness 2	_____ Commission Expires *(if not on seal)*
_____ Printed Name of Adult Witness 2	_____ Notary's County of Residence
_____ Date _____ Initial here if the Witnesses participated by phone.	

This advance directive was created by the Indiana Patient Preferences Coalition and is freely available. See www.INadvancedirectives.org for more information.

CHAPTER 12
FORM 6: LIVING WILL DECLARATION

IN FORM CAN REFUSE FURTHER MEDICAL CARE IF LATER FALL BADLY ILL

This form lets person say to stop most health care of <u>incapacitated person</u> if **later** <u>doctors think person has very bad health</u> and <u>more care likely won't help</u>. This long form is hard to read fast is more often used <u>inside</u> hospitals or similar places. This form is mostly done only by sickest or oldest people and most people skip this form. This form only matters if a person is later incapacitated. This book's form is based on an old form that use to be in state statues, but many doctors and nursing homes are familiar with this form.

FORM CAN SAY TO NOT GIVE CARE IF DOCTORS THINK IT WON'T HELP

This form lets person say health care should stop <u>if **later** doctors think person is in very bad health</u> and <u>more health care likely won't help</u>. The form lets people pick how bad must health be before form applies, and form also has other options to select. A doctor often helps explain form. Hospitals and similar may have their own form they prefer. After doing form a person with capacity is free to cancel it.

PERSON SIGNS FORM IN FRONT OF NOTARY OR 2 WITNESSES

To complete form a person signs in front of 2 witnesses who must be at least 18 and can't be spouse, parent, child, or any person financially responsible for the sick person's care, and also a witness should not be likely to benefit and get money or property from a person's Will or similar gift. The form usually should be shown to any doctor or facility that may give care to make it part of a person's medical file to follow. To cancel form a person should tell all persons and places shown the form it is canceled.

LIVING WILL DECLARATION

Declaration made this ___ day of _____ (month, year).

I, _____ , being at least eighteen (18) years of age and of sound mind, willfully and voluntarily make known my desires that my dying shall not be artificially prolonged under the circumstances set forth below, and I declare:

If at any time my attending physician certifies in writing that: (1) I have an incurable injury, disease, or illness; (2) my death will occur within a short time; and (3) the use of life prolonging procedures would serve only to artificially prolong the dying process, I direct that such procedures be withheld or withdrawn, and that I be permitted to die naturally with only the performance or provision of any medical procedure or medication necessary to provide me with comfort care or to alleviate pain, and, if I have so indicated below, the provision of artificially supplied nutrition and hydration. (Indicate your choice by initialing or making your mark before signing this declaration):

_____ I wish to receive artificially supplied nutrition and hydration, even if the effort to sustain life is futile or excessively burdensome to me.

_____ I do not wish to receive artificially supplied nutrition and hydration, if the effort to sustain life is futile or excessively burdensome to me.

_____ I intentionally make no decision concerning artificially supplied nutrition and hydration, leaving the decision to my health care representative including under IC 16-36-1-7 or my attorney in fact with health care powers including under IC 30-5-5.

Other instructions:_____
_____
_____
_____.

In the absence of my ability to give directions regarding the use of life prolonging procedures, it is my intention that this declaration be honored by my family and physician as the final expression of my legal right to refuse medical or surgical treatment and accept the consequences of the refusal.

I understand the full import of this declaration.

Signed _____

_____
City, County, and State of Residence

The declarant has been personally known to me, and I believe (him/her) to be of sound mind. I did not sign the declarant's signature above for or at the direction of the declarant. I am not a parent, spouse, or child of the declarant. I am not entitled to any part of the declarant's estate or directly financially responsible for the declarant's medical care. I am competent and at least eighteen (18) years of age.

Witness _____ Date _____

Witness _____ Date _____

CHAPTER 13
FORM 7: DO NOT RESUSCITATE

IN FORM CAN REFUSE HEALTH CARE STARTING IMMEDIATELY

The forms in this chapter say to immediately no longer try certain medical treatments listed in forms. This chapter covers 2 similar but different forms. These forms only matters if person is later incapacitated. These forms are mostly done only by very sick or very old people, and most people skip these forms. These forms are short and can be read fast by paramedics or similar so these forms can be used <u>outside</u> hospitals or similar places (these forms are often called "Out Of Hospital" forms), but these forms also are used inside hospitals or similar places too.

SAYS TO IMMEDIATELY NOT GIVE HEALTH CARE AS FORM EXPLAINS

Forms can say to <u>immediately</u> not try certain health care which is a very serious step rarely done.

First, the <u>"Do Not Resuscitate" form, often called the D.N.R. form, says to not try cardio-pulmonary resuscitation (C.P.R.)</u> to attempt to restart heart or breathing (by pressing chest and forcing air into mouth).

<u>Second, this chapter also provides the Physician Orders For Scope Of Treatment form</u>, often called the P.O.S.T form, which says to <u>not try many medical treatments listed</u> in form to pick from not just C.P.R. In other states this form has other names like P.O.L.S.T. form or M.O.S.T. form.

Pain relief and comfort care is still given so a person falling sick who did these forms is still usually taken to get this care. A person's doctor often helps select and fill out these forms.

FORM IS SIGNED BY PERSON AND PERSON'S DOCTOR

A form in this chapter must be signed by person and their doctor or similar. Note, the term "physician" is used in the forms which just means doctor. A form in this chapter once done should be shown to places that may give care to copy in a person's medical file. People often keep form nearby to show to paramedics or similar who may try to give some health care (like in pocket, on bedside table, taped on fridge, in wallet, or as part of a special bracelet). To cancel form a person usually should tell all places who saw the form. A person if not incapacitated can always change their mind, like by not showing these forms to paramedics, or by telling a nurse or doctor thing like, "Ignore my D-N-R, I now want all care". Most people tell family if they do these forms so they can inform doctors, paramedics, and others if needed.

STATE OF INDIANA
OUT OF HOSPITAL DO NOT RESUSCITATE DECLARATION AND ORDER
State Form 49559 (R / 9-11)

This declaration and order is effective on the date of execution and remains in effect until the death of the declarant or revocation.

OUT OF HOSPITAL DO NOT RESUSCITATE DECLARATION

Declaration made this _____ day of _____, _____, being of sound mind and at least eighteen (18) years of age, willfully and voluntarily make known my desires that my dying shall not be artificially prolonged under the circumstances set forth below.

I declare:
My attending physician has certified that I am a qualified person, meaning that I have a terminal condition or a medical condition such that, if I suffer cardiac or pulmonary failure, resuscitation would be unsuccessful or within a short period I would experience repeated cardiac or pulmonary failure resulting in death.

I direct that, if I experience cardiac or pulmonary failure in a location other than an acute care hospital, cardiopulmonary resuscitation procedures be withheld or withdrawn and that I be permitted to die naturally. My medical care may include any medical procedure necessary to provide me with comfort care or to alleviate pain.

I understand that I may revoke this Out of Hospital Do Not Resuscitate Declaration at any time by a signed and dated writing, by destroying or canceling this document, or by communicating to health care providers at the scene the desire to revoke this declaration.

I understand the full import of this declaration

Signature of declarant

Printed name of declarant

City and state of residence

The declarant is personally known to me, and I believe the declarant to be of sound mind. I did not sign the declarant's signature above, for, or at the direction of, the declarant. I am not a parent, spouse, or child of the declarant. I am not entitled to any part of the declarant's estate or directly financially responsible for the declarant's medical care. I am competent and at least eighteen (18) years of age.

Signature of witness	Printed name	Date *(month, day, year)*
Signature of witness	Printed name	Date *(month, day, year)*

OUT OF HOSPITAL DO NOT RESUSCITATE ORDER

I, _____, the attending physician of _____, have certified the declarant as a qualified person to make an Out Of Hospital Do Not Resuscitate Declaration, and I order health care providers having actual notice of this Out Of Hospital Do Not Resuscitate Declaration and Order not to initiate or continue cardiopulmonary resuscitation procedures on behalf of the declarant, unless the Out Of Hospital Do Not Resuscitate Declaration is revoked.

Signature of attending physician

Printed name of attending physician	Medical license number	Date *(month, day, year)*

THIS PAGE LEFT INTENTIONALLY BLANK

INDIANA PHYSICIAN ORDERS FOR SCOPE OF TREATMENT (POST)
State Form 55317 (R5 / 1-23)
Indiana Department of Health – IC 16-36-6

INSTRUCTIONS: This form is a physician's order for scope of treatment based on the patient's current medical condition and preferences. The POST should be reviewed whenever the patient's condition changes. A POST form is voluntary. A patient is not required to complete a POST form. A patient with capacity or their legal representative may void a POST form at any time by communicating that intent to the health care provider. Any section not completed does not invalidate the form and implies full treatment for that section. HIPAA permits disclosure to health care professionals as necessary for treatment. The original form is personal property of the patient. A facsimile, paper, or electronic copy of this form is a valid form.

Patient Last Name	Patient First Name	Middle Initial

Birth Date *(mm/dd/yyyy)*	Medical Record Number	Date Prepared *(mm/dd/yyyy)*

	DESIGNATION OF PATIENT'S PREFERENCES: The following sections (A through D) are the patient's current preferences for scope of treatment.
A Check One	**CARDIOPULMONARY RESUSCITATION (CPR):** Patient has no pulse AND is not breathing. ☐ Attempt Resuscitation / CPR ☐ Do Not Attempt Resuscitation / DNR When not in cardiopulmonary arrest, follow orders in **B, C** and **D**.
B Check One	**MEDICAL INTERVENTIONS:** If patient has pulse AND is breathing OR has pulse and is NOT breathing. ☐ <u>Comfort Measures (Allow Natural Death)</u>: Treatment Goal: Maximize comfort through symptom management. Relieve pain and suffering through the use of any medication by any route, positioning, wound care and other measures. Use oxygen, suction and manual treatment of airway obstruction as needed for comfort. Patient prefers no transfer to hospital for life-sustaining treatments. Transfer to hospital only if comfort needs cannot be met in current location. ☐ <u>Limited Additional Interventions</u>: Treatment Goal: Stabilization of medical condition. In addition to care described in Comfort Measures above, use medical treatment for stabilization, IV fluids (hydration) and cardiac monitor as indicated to stabilize medical condition. May use basic airway management techniques and non-invasive positive-airway pressure. Do not intubate. Transfer to hospital if indicated to manage medical needs or comfort. Avoid intensive care if possible. ☐ <u>Full Intervention</u>: Treatment Goal: Full interventions including life support measures in the intensive care unit. In addition to care described in Comfort Measures and Limited Additional Interventions above, use intubation, advanced airway interventions, and mechanical ventilation as indicated. Transfer to hospital and/or intensive care unit if indicated to meet medical needs.
C Check One	**ANTIBIOTICS:** ☐ Use antibiotics for infection only if comfort cannot be achieved fully through other means. ☐ Use antibiotics consistent with treatment goals.
D Check One	**ARTIFICIALLY ADMINISTERED NUTRITION:** Always offer food and fluid by mouth if feasible. ☐ No artificial nutrition. ☐ Defined trial period of artificial nutrition by tube. (Length of trial: _____ Goal: _____) ☐ Long-term artificial nutrition.
	OPTIONAL ADDITIONAL ORDERS:
	SIGNATURE PAGE: This form consists of two (2) pages. Both pages must be present. The following page includes signatures required for the POST form to be effective.

Patient Name:_____   Date of Birth *(mm/dd/yyyy)*:_____

E	**SIGNATURE OF PATIENT OR LEGALLY APPOINTED REPRESENTATIVE:** In order for the POST form to be effective, the patient or legally appointed representative must sign and date the form below.
	SIGNATURE OF PATIENT OR LEGALLY APPOINTED REPRESENTATIVE My signature below indicates that my physician or physician's designee discussed with me the above orders and the selected orders correctly represent my wishes.

Signature *(required by statute)*	Print Name *(required by statute)*	Date *(required by statute)* *(mm/dd/yyyy)*

F	**CONTACT INFORMATION FOR LEGALLY APPOINTED REPRESENTATIVE IN SECTION E** *(IF APPLICABLE)*: If the signature above is other than patient's, add contact information for the representative.

Relationship of representative identified in Section E if patient does not have capacity *(required by statute)*	Address *(number and street, city, state, and ZIP code)*	Telephone Number

PHYSICIAN ORDER:

A POST form may be executed only by an individual's treating physician, advanced practice registered nurse, or physician assistant, and only if:

    (1) the treating physician, advanced practice registered nurse, or physician assistant has determined that:
        (A) the individual is a qualified person; and
        (B) the medical orders contained in the individual's POST form are reasonable and medically appropriate for the individual; and
    (2) the qualified person or representative has signed and dated the POST form

A qualified person is an individual who has at least one (1) of the following:
    (1) An advanced chronic progressive illness.
    (2) An advanced chronic progressive frailty.
    (3) A condition caused by injury, disease, or illness from which, to a reasonable degree of medical certainty:
        (A) there can be no recovery; and
        (B) death will occur from the condition within a short period without the provision of life prolonging procedures.
    (4) A medical condition that, if the person were to suffer cardiac or pulmonary failure, resuscitation would be unsuccessful or within a short period the person would experience repeated cardiac or pulmonary failure resulting in death.

G	**DOCUMENTATION OF DISCUSSION:** Orders discussed with *(check one)*: ☐ Patient (patient has capacity) ☐ Health Care Representative ☐ Legal Guardian ☐ Parent of Minor ☐ Health Care Power of Attorney
H	**SIGNATURE OF TREATING PHYSICIAN / ADVANCED PRACTICE REGISTERED NURSE / PHYSICIAN ASSISTANT** My signature below indicates that I or my designee have discussed with the patient or patient's representative the patient's goals and treatment options available to the patient based on the patient's health. My signature below indicates to the best of my knowledge that these orders are consistent with the patient's current medical condition and preferences.

Signature of Treating Physician / APRN / PA *(required by statute)*	Print Treating Physician / APRN / PA Name *(required by statute)*	Date *(required by statute)* *(mm/dd/yyyy)*
Physician / APRN / PA office telephone number *(required by statute)*	Physician / APRN / PA License Number *(required by statute)*	Health Care Professional preparing form if other than the physician / APRN / PA

I	**APPOINTMENT OF HEALTH CARE REPRESENTATIVE:** As a patient you have the option to appoint a representative to serve as your health care representative pursuant to IC 16-36-7. You are not required to designate a health care representative for this POST form to be effective. You are encouraged to consult with your attorney or other qualified individual about advance directives that are available to you. Forms and additional information about advance directives may be found on the IDOH web site at https://www.in.gov/health/cshcr/indiana-health-care-quality-resource-center/advance-directives-resource-center/ .

CHAPTER 14
FORM 8: POWER OF ATTORNEY

FORM LETS POWER BE GIVEN OVER PROPERTY, MONEY, AND MORE

This form lets person give power to someone to do things with person's money, property, and more. Some people this form a "Financial Power Of Attorney".

FORM GIVES POWER TO LET SOMEONE CONTROL PROPERTY AND MONEY

Form lets person give power to someone to do actions involving their money, property, and other things. Often named to get power is trusted person like spouse, relative, or friend. In a Power of Attorney document the person giving power is called "Principal", and person getting power called "Attorney in Fact" or "Agent". Giving power to someone can let them help by moving money in accounts, paying bills, buying or selling items, signing contracts, taking out debt, and getting information. This form might help if person is sick, busy, or away, and may avoid need for nursing home or unwanted legal action. A person who did form if still rational and not incapacitated can always overrule or fire an Attorney-in-Fact <u>so really power is shared</u>. The form is durable which means the form still has power even if person who did form later is incapacitated. Naming a second fallback person to act is rarely needed so it is rarely done. If using this form a signature should be like: "Ed Doe signing as Attorney-in-Fact under a Power of Attorney for Ann Wu".

IN FORM INITIAL LINES TO PICK POWERS THAT ARE GIVEN

In form are spots to initial to say which powers are given. But most people give all or most powers since they trust person getting power and a bank or similar may not follow form if power given is not clear.

DUE TO RISKS INCLUDING FRAUD MANY SKIP FORM OR CONSULT A LAWYER

Doing this form can be risky and lead to loss of money and property since an Attorney-in-Fact can do dumb or criminal actions like wasting money on dumb items, causing harm by carelessness, or stealing. There is a legal duty to act reasonably and an Attorney-in-Fact can be sued later, but they might be out of money so can't undo their harm. Usually banks or others can't be blamed for obeying an Attorney-in-Fact. This area of law is complex and basic acts may be fine like paying bills, moving funds, or getting records -- but less usual acts may be improper or criminal like making big gifts to family or friends, making unusual or risky investments, or doing unusual acts. Many people ask a lawyer for advice about this form.

PERSON SIGNS FORM IN FRONT OF A NOTARY

The form must be signed by person in front of a notary. Once completed a person can keep form on hand ready to hand out, but many people quickly give form to person getting power to use if later needed. Some cautious people quickly show form to banks or similar to explain they should later follow the form. To cancel form a person should take back copies and usually tell all places shown the form it's canceled.

POWER OF ATTORNEY

NOTICE: THE POWERS GRANTED BY THIS DOCUMENT ARE BROAD AND SWEEPING. THEY ARE DEFINED BY INDIANA CODE SECTION 30-5-5-2 AND RELATED LAWS. IF YOU HAVE QUESTIONS OBTAIN LEGAL ADVICE. THIS DOCUMENT MAY BE REVOKED BY YOU IF YOU LATER WISH TO DO SO. THIS DOCUMENT AUTHORIZES ANOTHER PERSON TO ACT FOR YOU.

I, _____ (name and address) appoint _____ (name and address) as my attorney-in-fact to act for me in any lawful way with respect to the following initialed subjects, as each subject is defined and described in the Indiana Code, which is incorporated by reference herein:

INITIALS

_____ a. Real property transactions (Indiana Code § 30-5-5-2), including but not limited to the following real property: _____
_____ b. Tangible personal property transactions (Indiana Code § 30-5-5-3)
_____ c. Bond, share and commodity transactions (Indiana Code § 30-5-5-4)
_____ d. Retirement plans (Indiana Code § 30-5-5-4.5)
_____ e. Banking transactions (Indiana Code § 30-5-5-5)
_____ f. Business operating transactions (Indiana Code § 30-5-5-6)
_____ g. Insurance transactions (Indiana Code § 30-5-5-7)
_____ h. Beneficiary transactions (Indiana Code § 30-5-5-8)
_____ i. Gift transactions (Indiana Code § 30-5-5-9)
_____ j. Fiduciary transactions (Indiana Code § 30-5-5-10)
_____ k. Claims and litigation (Indiana Code § 30-5-5-11)
_____ l. Family maintenance (Indiana Code § 30-5-5-12)
_____ m. Benefits from military service (Indiana Code § 30-5-5-13)
_____ n. Records, reports, and statements (Indiana Code § 30-5-5-14)
_____ o. Estate transactions (Indiana Code § 30-5-5-15)
_____ p. Delegation of authority (Indiana Code § 30-5-5-18)
_____ q. General authority as to all other matters (Indiana Code § 30-5-5-19)

Special Instructions: (you may give special instructions extending or limiting the powers you granted to the attorney-in-fact in the following area) _____
_____
_____.

This power of attorney is effective immediately and shall not be terminated or affected by my disability, incapacity, incompetence, or by lapse of time (or uncertainty as to my condition or about revocation).

I agree any third party who receives a copy of this document may act under it, I agree revocation of this power of attorney is not effective as to a third party until they learn of revocation, and I agree to indemnify any third party for claims that arise because of reliance of this power of attorney.

Signed this ____ day of _____, 20___.

_____   _____
Signature of Principal   Printed Name of Principal

State of _____, County of _____ } ss
Before me, the undersigned, a Notary Public in and for said county and state, personally appeared _____, who acknowledged the execution of the foregoing Power of Attorney.

Witness my hand and notarial seal this ____ day of _____, 20____.

My commission expires: _____   _____
My county of residence: _____   Signature of Notary Public
                                                                           Printed Name of Notary Public: _____

CHAPTER 15
FORM 9: DELEGATION TO CONSENT TO HEALTH CARE OF MINOR CHILD

FORM LETS PARENT GIVE POWER OVER HEALTH CARE OF MINOR CHILD
This form lets parent give power to control health care of a minor child under 18 to someone.

FORM GIVES SOMEONE POWER OVER CHILD'S HEALTH CARE
In this form a parent can delegate to the person named in the form over control of a child's health care. This form can let friend, relative, or teacher control a child's health care if needed. This form is often used if parent or child is away from the other for work, school, sports, drug treatment, prison or jail, immigration, military, month long visit, or if child is sick in hospital and needs person close by. The form is not done for minor situations like a babysitter or short visits. Using this form may avoid need for serious court action. A parent can cancel form, overrule any decision, and fire the person given power <u>so really power is shared</u>.

FORM IS SIGNED BY PARENT IN FRONT OF 1 WITNESS
The form must be signed by a parent in front of 1 witness who is an adult. The form can be modified to add second parent if wanted. The form can be modified to let a legal guardian share power with someone. The form when completed can be kept by parent until needed but often is quickly given to person named to get power to use if needed. Some cautious parents quickly show form to schools and doctors so they know to follow it later. To cancel form a person should take back all copies and usually tell all places shown the form it's canceled. Usually a form is done for each child but it can be modified to cover several children.

DELEGATION TO CONSENT TO HEALTH CARE OF MINOR CHILD

I, who am the parent of the minor child named _____ born on _____ do **appoint the following person to have power and authority to control and consent to health care of any kind** for this minor child, including hospitalization and transportation related to health care:

Person receiving power

    Name:_____
    Address:_____
    Phone numbers:_____

This document allows the person getting power to do all things necessary or helpful to the child's health care, and this includes but is not limited to the he following powers:

1. All medical, dental, and other health related matters. This includes consenting to medical treatment and ability to receive records. They shall have all authority described in Indiana Code 30-5-5-16, and they are hereby appointed as the health care representative for the child.

2. All matters related to Medicaid, Hoosier Healthwise, or any other health insurance, and all other benefits for the child. The person getting power in this document is hereby appointed to receive all related benefits on behalf of the child.

3. The person getting power is given power to travel with the child.

4. Any and all other actions necessary for the care and benefit of the child related to health.

This document is effective immediately when signed but expires after 12 months.

This document is done under Indiana law including Indiana Code 16-36-1-5 and 16-36-1-6.

I order the person getting power in this document should have access to all relevant medical information about the child.

I understand as a parent I may be responsible for all medical expenses incurred.

Parent

    Signature of Parent:_____ Date:_____
    Address:_____
    Phone numbers:_____

Witness

    Signature of Witness:_____ Date:_____

CHAPTER 16
FORM 10: FUNERAL PLANNING DECLARATION

LETS PERSON BE NAMED TO CONTROL FUNERAL AND RELATED MATTERS
Form lets person be named to control funeral and related matters like burial, cremation, and events. This book's form is a statutory form found in Indiana law.

CAN NAME PERSON TO CONTROL DEAD BODY AND GIVE INSTRUCTIONS
Form lets person give power to someone called the "designee" to control funeral and related things like the bodily remains, burial, cremation, ceremonies, tombstone, and buying goods and services for all this. If form is not done by law control is by closest family (spouse, adult child, parents, then brothers or sisters). People do this form rarely usually if it seems family may be too upset while mourning, be bad with money, or do unwanted things. Payment for things will come from pre-paid funeral accounts, insurance, and the decedent's or estate's money and property, and Executor and family legally must help arrange payment. The form has spots for options and instructions but many people skip this and just trust the person selected or family to do what they verbally said they wanted. People including family legally should do funeral, burial, and related things the deceased wanted if decedent's properly, money, and estate can afford it.

SEVERAL OPTIONS ABOUT BODILY REMAINS AND EVENTS EXIST
After a death police are told and funeral home or crematorium come get body. Half of people pick burial and half cremation. If picking cremation later "cremains" go to family or "columbarium" vault in cemetery.

Half of people do not do early events in first month when shocked family may be unready for visitors. Importantly, if "Direct Burial" or "Direct Cremation" is requested costs might be 80% off usual $10,000+ but this skips events with body till after burial or cremation in week or so. Weeks or months later people may do ash scattering, ceremony, or dinner at park, house, church, or hall, often with food, speech, or video.

Half of people do early events within month, and there are several different options to pick from. First, some people do within days a "Vigil", "Viewing", or "Wake", where family and friends talk or pray maybe in room with body (with closed or open casket) or cremated ashes, often at Funeral Home or church. Second, some people do big ceremony within week of either a) funeral (maybe with Mass) in church with priest or minister, or b) informal event like "Celebration of Life" or "Remembrance" with or without the body. Third, some people do final event at cemetery (religious or not), like a burial or putting ashes in a vault. Note, if event uses body not just ashes it usually is at funeral home, church, or cemetery and within weeks.

SIGN FORM WITH NOTARY AND 2 WITNESSES
The form must be signed by person in front of 2 witnesses who then sign form. Witnesses should be at least 18 and not parent, spouse, or child of person doing the form or a spouse of any of these people. Witnesses should not be entitled or expecting to benefit from the person's death or estate. To cancel the form a person should take back all copies and then usually tell all places shown the form it's canceled.

FUNERAL PLANNING DECLARATION

(Indiana Code 29-2-19-9)

Declaration made this _____ day of _____ (month, year).

I, _____, being at least eighteen (18) years of age and of sound mind, willfully and voluntarily make known my instructions concerning funeral services, ceremonies, and the disposition of my remains after my death.

I hereby declare and direct that after my death _____ (name of designee) shall, as my designee, carry out the instructions that are set forth in this declaration. If my designee is unwilling or unable to act, I nominate _____ as an alternate designee.

I hereby declare and direct that after my death the following actions be taken (indicate your choice by initialing or making your mark before signing this declaration):

(1) My body shall be:
    (A) _____ Buried. I direct that my body be buried at _____
_____.
    (B) _____ Cremated. I direct that my cremated remains be disposed of as follows: _____
_____.
    (C) _____ Entombed. I direct that my body be entombed at _____
_____.
    (D) _____ I intentionally make no decision concerning the disposition of my body, leaving the decision to my designee (as named above).

(2) My arrangements shall be made as follows:
    (A) I direct that funeral services be obtained from: _____
_____.
    (B) I direct that the following ceremonial arrangements be made: _____
_____.
    (C) I direct the selection of a grave memorial that: _____
_____.
    (D) I direct that the following merchandise and other property be selected for the disposition of my remains, my funeral or other ceremonial arrangements:
_____
_____
_____.

(E) _____ I direct that my designee (as named above) make all arrangements concerning ceremonies and other funeral services.

(3) In addition to the instructions listed above, I request the following: _____
_____
_____
_____
_____
_____.

(4) If it is impossible to make an arrangement specified in subdivisions (1) through (3) because:
    (A) a funeral home or other service provider is out of business, impossible to locate, or otherwise unable to provide the specified service; or
    (B) the specified arrangement is impossible, impractical, or illegal;
I direct my designee to make alternate arrangements to the best of the designee's ability.

It is my intention that this declaration be honored by my family and others as the final expression of my intentions concerning my funeral and the disposition of my body after my death. I understand the full import of this declaration.

    Signed _____

_____
City, County, and State of Residence

The declarant is personally known to me, and I believe the declarant to be of sound mind. I did not sign the declarant's signature above for or at the direction of the declarant. I am not a parent, spouse, or child of the declarant. I am not entitled to any part of the declarant's estate. I am competent and at least eighteen (18) years of age.

    Witness _____   Date _____

    Witness _____   Date _____

APPENDIX: SAMPLE FILLED OUT FORMS

TO GET FORMS TO USE PEOPLE CAN:
   (1) PHOTOCOPY BOOK PAGES,
   (2) TEAR OUT PAGES FROM A BOOK, OR
   (3) DOWNLOAD BOOK WITH FORMS FROM WWW.DAVENPORTPUBLISHING.COM
AND USUALLY PDF FORM AT IS BEST TO AVOID SPACING/FORMAT CHANGES.

EMAIL ANY COMMENTS TO DAVENPORTPRESS@GMAIL.COM.

On the next pages to show how it can be done are some sample filled out legal forms.

People can add words to legal forms by computer or typewriter to be neater, but many people just by hand use pen, marker, or pencil to handwrite words into forms.

It is not required but is bit better if signatures are in ink or marker not pencil.

Many parts of the forms especially Will gifts can be left empty and unfilled.

Anyone can fill in words in legal form not just the person doing the form, like a friend with neat writing can fill in all the words, addresses, and dates that are needed. Only the final signatures must be done by each person who wants the form.

To add words in form by pen, pencil, typewriter, or computer any of these is fine:
       "I appoint _*John Doe*_ as Agent",
       "I appoint ___John Doe___ as Agent",
       "I appoint John Doe as Agent".

When doing forms it may help to know "respectively" means "in order just stated".

People need not worry about neatness or small mistakes, and a document is usually fine if those people who knew a decedent in life can tell the likely meaning.

**Sample Filled Out Form: Last Will and Testament (Standard)
with Gifts section skipped to not bother with this**

LAST WILL AND TESTAMENT

I, *Susan Lee Maxwell*, of *Lake* County, Indiana, do revoke all prior Wills, Testaments, and Codicils, and do make, publish, and declare this to be my Will. When doing this I am of sound mind and under no duress or undue influence.

1. GIFTS. I give these gifts in this Will, but to get a gift in this section the recipient must survive me except as otherwise stated below.

I give _____ to _____.

I give _____ to _____.

I give _____ to _____.

I give _____ to _____.

I give _____ to _____.

I give _____ to _____.

I give _____ to _____.

I give _____ to _____.

I give _____ to _____.

I give _____ to _____.

I give _____ to _____.

[SKIPPED written across gift lines]

2. GIFTS OF TANGIBLE PERSONAL PROPERTY BY SEPARATE WRITINGS. I may gift tangible personal property by writings separate from a Will. Such a writing not found within 90 days of my death is canceled and of no effect. Such a writing existing when this Will is done is not revoked or canceled unless this Will specifically says this.

3. RESIDUE. I give the rest and residue and remainder of my estate, my money and property of any kind and nature, and anything I have an interest in so long as it was not transferred by other Will provisions (all of which is called the "residue"), as follows:

   a) to *Paul Thomas Maxwell* who survive me with persons just named who survive me taking the share of non-survivors, then

   b) to *Jennifer Pamela Maxwell and Oscar Tabor* and if any of those just named do not survive me their part goes to their lineal descendants, per stirpes.

4. ADMINISTRATION. I name and appoint *Paul Thomas Maxwell* as Personal Representative including for me, my Will, and my estate.

5. MISCELLANEOUS. The following applies to this Will and generally.

   Priority of Will gifts of the same type is based on the order they are written.

   In this document no unfilled part is a mistake and residue spaces may be left blank.

   The words "give" and "gift" also means a devise, bequest, grant, legacy, or similar.

   A gift of property no longer owned by Testator at death shall lapse and be of no effect including no payment of money shall be done in its place, all without ademption.

   If gift or gift section mentions survival, survive, or surviving then survival is an absolute condition and anti-lapse laws or similar have no effect.

   Any failure to make gifts to family including children is intentional and not a mistake.

   No gift or transfer made during life reduces or offsets a Will gift unless during my life I expressly usually called it a "loan" or "advancement".

   Use of particular gender shall include other genders, reference to singular or plural shall be interchangeable, and "they" may be singular or plural.

   Unless parts of this Will specifically says otherwise a secured debt like mortgage or lien on real property or vehicles shall not be paid off, recipient of property takes it subject to liens, and no recipient who has debtor take property or get payment via use or threat of a secured debt may require a devisee, recipient, heir, or estate to pay or do anything.

   I give any Personal Representative a) the fullest authority, powers, and discretion allowed by state law, b) authority to lease, sell, mortgage, convey, or retain property including real property in any such manner and time they deem helpful or proper, and c) authority to anytime pay or settle claims or debts if they in their sole discretion chooses.

   Any Personal Representative shall not be required to render and file annual or other accountings with respect to property or money including in relation to my Will or estate. Any Personal Representative may act independently in all ways without supervision.

I request informal or administrative probate of my Will and estate without supervision.

If context permits the terms Personal Representative, Executor, and Administrator shall be seen as interchangeable as if all were written, and if context permits the term Guardian of the Estate is interchangeable with Guardian of Property and Conservator.

The residue includes lapsed or failed gifts, insurance paid to estate, inheritances owed me, and property I had a power of appointment or testamentary disposition over.

Any Personal Representative, Executor, Guardian of any kind, Conservator, and any fiduciary under this Will or otherwise, shall qualify and serve without bond, security, surety, or similar, including despite place of residence or lack of ties to a state or country.

A Guardian of any kind should serve all persons without full capacity in my care.

This Will does not revoke a Living Will or any legal document concerning health care.

A Personal Representative using their sole discretion has power at any time to transfer a minor child's money or property to person named Guardian of the Estate in Will to serve as Custodian under the Indiana Uniform Transfers to Minors Act or similar law here or in other states, to serve until minor is 18, all without bond our any court action. If they are unable to serve the person named Personal Representative in Will shall be Custodian.

TESTATOR

IN WITNESS WHEREOF, I, the Testator doing this Will, do now sign, declare, and publish this document as my Will, this _22nd_ day of _June_, 20_22_.

Susan Lee Maxwell
Testator signature

WITNESSES

We, the Witnesses who are named below, say the Testator named above did sign, declare, and publish this document as the Testator's Will when he appeared to be of sound mind and acting voluntarily and not under duress, and we the Witnesses in Testator's presence and presence of each other have hereunto signed our names acting as witnesses on the _22nd_ day of _June_, 20_22_.

Eve Mable Rogers   _24 2nd St., Bond, IN 46882_
Witness   Address

Mary Ann Moon   _14 2nd St., Chicago, IL 66018_
Witness   Address

**Sample Filled Out Form: Last Will and Testament (Standard)
with Residue Clause using percentages**

LAST WILL AND TESTAMENT

I, ___Ruth May Kent___, of ___Marion___ County, Indiana, do revoke all prior Wills, Testaments, and Codicils, and do make, publish, and declare this to be my Will. When doing this I am of sound mind and under no duress or undue influence.

1. GIFTS. I give these gifts in this Will, but to get a gift in this section the recipient must survive me except as otherwise stated below.

I give _big oak table_ to _Anne J. Wix._

I give _$5,000_ to _Loretta Marsha Switt_ in the hope she will help herself and her _young daughters Megan and Pamela_ .

I give _63 Ivy Road, Indianapolis, Indiana_ to _Kenneth Victor Poppler._

I give _all land in Allen County in Indiana state_ to _Greta Olivia Fox._

I give _all land in Harris County in Texas state_ to _Wanda Evelyn Fox._

I give _9087 Wilderness Road, Bozeman, MT_ to _James Eric Hanson_ .

I give _Bronze Roman Lamp_ to _Anne Kilby_ and _Kevin Kilby._

I give _wedding ring_ to _Ruth Jones._

I give _all jewelry not given above_ to _Kay Pidoski._

I give _$7,281.35_ to _Wanda Kay Zinski_ .

I give _UBank account #8980443723_ to _Joy Rundy a fishing buddy_ .

I give _Wells Fargo acct ending in #8923_ to _Lawrence Deer_ .

I give _1998 Ford truck_ to _John Rupert Smith_ .

I give _a total of $50,000_ to _Brian Peterson, Michael Peterson, and Mary Hart_

I give _$1,000_ to _that charity food kitchen on Smith Avenue in Evansville, IN._

I give _all spare tires and auto parts I own_ to _Victor Perez my mechanic_ .

I give _$6,000 in total_ to _my cousin Carol Brown's children_ .

I give _$1000 each_ to _each of my grandchildren_ .

2. GIFTS OF TANGIBLE PERSONAL PROPERTY BY SEPARATE WRITINGS.
I may gift tangible personal property by writings separate from a Will. Such a writing not found within 90 days of my death is canceled and of no effect. Such a writing existing when this Will is done is not revoked or canceled unless this Will specifically says this.

3. RESIDUE. I give the rest and residue and remainder of my estate, my property of any kind and nature, and anything I have an interest in (all of which is called the "residue"), so long as any such thing was not transferred by other Will provisions, as follows:
  a) to _____Pamela Bonnie Ford my wife_____ who survive me with persons just named who survive me taking the share of non-survivors, then
  b) to 40% to Paul Brian Ford, 40% to Karen Lisa Ford, and 20% to Pedro Juan Sanchez and if any of those just named do not survive me their part goes to their lineal descendants, per stirpes.

4. ADMINISTRATION. I name and appoint ___Pamela Bonnie Ford___ as Personal Representative including for me, my Will, and my estate.

5. MISCELLANEOUS. The following applies to this Will and generally.
  Priority of Will gifts of the same type is based on the order they are written.
  In this document no unfilled part is a mistake and residue spaces may be left blank.
  The words "give" and "gift" also means a devise, bequest, grant, legacy, or similar.
  A gift of property no longer owned by Testator at death shall lapse and be of no effect including no payment of money shall be done in its place, all without ademption.
  If gift or gift section mentions survival, survive, or surviving then survival is an absolute condition and anti-lapse laws or similar have no effect.
  Any failure to make gifts to family including children is intentional and not a mistake.
  No gift or transfer made during life reduces or offsets a Will gift unless during my life I expressly usually called it a "loan" or "advancement".
  Use of particular gender shall include other genders, reference to singular or plural shall be interchangeable, and "they" may be singular or plural.
  Unless parts of this Will specifically says otherwise a secured debt like mortgage or lien on real property or vehicles shall not be paid off, recipient of property takes it subject to liens, and no recipient who has debtor take property or get payment via use or threat of a secured debt may require a devisee, recipient, heir, or estate to pay or do anything.
  I give any Personal Representative a) the fullest authority, powers, and discretion allowed by state law, b) authority to lease, sell, mortgage, convey, or retain property including real property in any such manner and time they deem helpful or proper, and c) authority to anytime pay or settle claims or debts if they in their sole discretion chooses.
  Any Personal Representative shall not be required to render and file annual or other

accountings with respect to property or money including in relation to my Will or estate. Any Personal Representative may act independently in all ways without supervision.

I request informal or administrative probate of my Will and estate without supervision.

If context permits the terms Personal Representative, Executor, and Administrator shall be seen as interchangeable as if all were written, and if context permits the term Guardian of the Estate is interchangeable with Guardian of Property and Conservator.

The residue includes lapsed or failed gifts, insurance paid to estate, inheritances owed me, and property I had a power of appointment or testamentary disposition over.

Any Personal Representative, Executor, Guardian of any kind, Conservator, and any fiduciary under this Will or otherwise, shall qualify and serve without bond, security, surety, or similar, including despite place of residence or lack of ties to a state or country.

A Guardian of any kind should serve all persons without full capacity in my care.

This Will does not revoke a Living Will or any legal document concerning health care.

A Personal Representative using their sole discretion has power at any time to transfer a minor child's money or property to person named Guardian of the Estate in Will to serve as Custodian under the Indiana Uniform Transfers to Minors Act or similar law here or in other states, to serve until minor is 18, all without bond our any court action. If they are unable to serve the person named Personal Representative in Will shall be Custodian.

TESTATOR

IN WITNESS WHEREOF, I, the Testator doing this Will, do now sign, declare, and publish this document as my Will, this __30th__ day of __December__, 20 __09__.

Henry James Ford
Testator signature

WITNESSES

We, the Witnesses who are named below, say the Testator named above did sign, declare, and publish this document as the Testator's Will when he appeared to be of sound mind and acting voluntarily and not under duress, and we the Witnesses in Testator's presence and presence of each other have hereunto signed our names acting as witnesses on the __30th__ day of __December__, 20 __09__.

__Olivia Joy Pawlenty__   87 Hastings Avenue, Buffalo, IN 46987
Witness   Address

__Roy Felix Pawlenty__   87 Hastings Avenue, Buffalo, IN 46987
Witness   Address

**Sample Filled Out Form: Last Will and Testament (Standard)
with Gifts section mostly skipped and Will modified to have 1 Part Residue Clause**

LAST WILL AND TESTAMENT

I, **David Eric Smith**, of **Tippecanoe** County, Indiana, do revoke all prior Wills, Testaments, and Codicils, and do make, publish, and declare this to be my Will. When doing this I am of sound mind and under no duress or undue influence.

1. GIFTS. I give these gifts in this Will, but to get a gift in this section the recipient must survive me except as otherwise stated below.

| I give | $500 | to | each of my brothers, sisters, and cousins | . |

| I give | $1000 | to | Baker Food Shelf in Fort Wayne, Indiana | . |

2. GIFTS OF TANGIBLE PERSONAL PROPERTY BY SEPARATE WRITINGS. I may gift tangible personal property by writings separate from a Will. Such a writing not found within 90 days of my death is canceled and of no effect. Such a writing existing when this Will is done is not revoked or canceled unless this Will specifically says this.

3. RESIDUE. The rest and residue and remainder of my estate, my property of any kind and nature, and anything I have an interest in, I give to **Ann Sue Baker and Adam Michael Smith who survive me** and to lineal descendants per stirpes of a person just named who did not survive me.

4. ADMINISTRATION. I name and appoint **Ann Sue Baker** as Personal Representative including for me, my Will, and my estate.

5. MISCELLANEOUS. The following applies to this Will and generally.
Priority of Will gifts of the same type is based on the order they are written.
In this document no unfilled part is a mistake and residue spaces may be left blank.
The words "give" and "gift" also means a devise, bequest, grant, legacy, or similar.
A gift of property no longer owned by Testator at death shall lapse and be of no effect including no payment of money shall be done in its place, all without ademption.
If gift or gift section mentions survival, survive, or surviving then survival is an absolute condition and anti-lapse laws or similar have no effect.
Any failure to make gifts to family including children is intentional and not a mistake.

No gift or transfer made during life reduces or offsets a Will gift unless during my life I expressly usually called it a "loan" or "advancement".

Use of particular gender shall include other genders, reference to singular or plural shall be interchangeable, and "they" may be singular or plural.

Unless parts of this Will specifically says otherwise a secured debt like mortgage or lien on real property or vehicles shall not be paid off, recipient of property takes it subject to liens, and no recipient who has debtor take property or get payment via use or threat of a secured debt may require a devisee, recipient, heir, or estate to pay or do anything.

I give any Personal Representative a) the fullest authority, powers, and discretion allowed by state law, b) authority to lease, sell, mortgage, convey, or retain property including real property in any such manner and time they deem helpful or proper, and c) authority to anytime pay or settle claims or debts if they in their sole discretion chooses.

Any Personal Representative shall not be required to render and file annual or other accountings with respect to property or money including in relation to my Will or estate. Any Personal Representative may act independently in all ways without supervision.

I request informal or administrative probate of my Will and estate without supervision.

If context permits the terms Personal Representative, Executor, and Administrator shall be seen as interchangeable as if all were written, and if context permits the term Guardian of the Estate is interchangeable with Guardian of Property and Conservator.

The residue includes lapsed or failed gifts, insurance paid to estate, inheritances owed me, and property I had a power of appointment or testamentary disposition over.

Any Personal Representative, Executor, Guardian of any kind, Conservator, and any fiduciary under this Will or otherwise, shall qualify and serve without bond, security, surety, or similar, including despite place of residence or lack of ties to a state or country.

A Guardian of any kind should serve all persons without full capacity in my care.

This Will does not revoke a Living Will or any legal document concerning health care.

A Personal Representative using their sole discretion has power at any time to transfer a minor child's money or property to person named Guardian of the Estate in Will to serve as Custodian under the Indiana Uniform Transfers to Minors Act or similar law here or in other states, to serve until minor is 18, all without bond our any court action. If they are unable to serve the person named Personal Representative in Will shall be Custodian.

TESTATOR

IN WITNESS WHEREOF, I, the Testator doing this Will, do now sign, declare, and publish this document as my Will, this _21st_ day of _June_, 20_21_.

David Eric Smith
Testator signature

WITNESSES

We, the Witnesses who are named below, say the Testator named above did sign, declare, and publish this document as the Testator's Will when he appeared to be of sound mind and acting voluntarily and not under duress, and we the Witnesses in Testator's presence and presence of each other have hereunto signed our names acting as witnesses on the _21st_ day of _June_, 20_21_.

Harriet Potter   204 Main Street, Buffalo, IN 46451
Witness signature   Witness address

Pamela Bonnie Rooker   83 River Road, Lakeville, IN 46028
Witness signature   Witness address

Sample Filled Out Form: Self-Proving Clause

SELF-PROVING CLAUSE

We, the undersigned Testator and the undersigned Witnesses, respectively, whose names are signed to the attached or foregoing instrument declare:

(1) that the Testator executed the instrument as the Testator's Will;

(2) that, in the presence of both Witnesses, the Testator signed or acknowledged the signature already made or directed another to sign for the Testator in the Testator's presence;

(3) that the Testator executed the Will as a free and voluntary act for the purposes expressed in it;

(4) that each of the Witnesses, in the presence of the Testator and of each other, signed the will as a Witness;

(5) that the Testator was of sound mind when the Will was executed; and

(6) that to the best knowledge of each of the Witnesses the Testator was, at the time the Will was executed, at least 18 years of age or was a member of the armed forces or of the merchant marine of the United States or its allies.

June 21, 2021
Date

David Eric Smith
Testator

Harriet Potter
Witness

Pamela Bonnie Rooker
Witness

Sample Filled Out Form: Tangible Personal Property List

TANGIBLE PERSONAL PROPERTY LIST

In this writing are gifts of tangible personal property to occur at my death of things not specifically disposed of by my Will.

A writing not found within 90 days of my death shall have no effect.

I may do many pages of these writings at different times and they all should be seen as 1 document, and if any conflicts occur the more recently done page controls.

If a person getting a gift below does not survive me such gift shall lapse and instead that property passes as my Will says including by Will residue clause.

PROPERTY ITEMS		NAMES OF RECIPIENTS
1998 Ford Truck	to	Samantha Bell
1.3 carat diamond ring + Irish rings	to	Ann Sue Reed
14 ft power boat + kayak + paddles	to	L. Wheeler
Parkhurst style bench	to	Reba Stewart
glass table, telescope, all umbrellas	to	Rebecca Stewart
18 wood cups, oak platter, oak vase	to	Mary and Cindy Lott
my wedding dress and shoes	to	Mary Lott
chainsaw marked with 382937	to	Mary Lott
chainsaw marked with 89930	to	Matt Smith
antique lanterns + repair kits	to	Sue Wu maid at Hart Hotel
oak lamp kept on porch	to	Mary Kay Poppler
sewing machines	to	Mary Kay Poppler
rocking chair bought in Oregon	to	Don Winkler boat mechanic
all fishing poles and fishing nets	to	Joe "Fish" Hoss, fishing pal
hats at cabin	to	Ken Baker
	to	
	to	

DATE: 2-12-2023   SIGNED: *David Eric Smith*

www.ingramcontent.com/pod-product-compliance
Lightning Source LLC
Chambersburg PA
CBHW080925220526
45465CB00008BA/2938